Route 66 Paranormal Alliance members. *From left to right*: Dustin Rowlett, Andrew Muller, Alicia Holder (seated, co-founder), Janice Tremeear (co-founder/author, standing), Dean Pestana, Kenneth Brewer (seated), Charlene Wells and Jeanna Barker. *Photo by Chris Bryant of Bryant Business Graphics, Buffalo, Missouri.*

HAUNTED OZARKS

JANICE TREMEEAR

Haunted America

Published by Haunted America
A Division of The History Press
Charleston, SC 29403
www.historypress.net

Manufactured in the United States

ISBN 978.1.60949.152.9

Library of Congress Cataloging-in-Publication Data

Tremeear, Janice.
Haunted Ozarks / Janice Tremeear.
p. cm.
Includes bibliographical references (p.   ).
ISBN 978-1-60949-152-9
1. Haunted places--Ozark Mountains. 2. Ghosts--Ozark Mountains. I. Title.
BF1472.U6T758 2011
133.109767'1--dc22
2011005033

A stone with a hole in it placed in the stable prevents horses from being ridden by witches at night. Braiding a horse's tail with ribbons prevents witches from riding it at night.

All mirrors in a room where a person has died should be covered, as the next person to look in the mirror will also die. A picture falling off the wall, a bird flying into the house and ringing in the ears all are signs of impending death.

To rid your house of ghosts, when you go to bed at night, set out the shoes you'll wear in the morning at the foot of the bed. Place one with the toes pointing one way and the other with the toes pointing the opposite way. This confuses the ghosts so badly that they will leave after a few nights.

Placing a tomato on your windowsill will scare away evil spirits. A tomato placed over the hearth will bring prosperity into the house. Tomato juice on your hair will make it grow faster. Tomatoes are considered an aphrodisiac and are called "Love Apples." (I often heard this term as a kid.) German folklore believed tomatoes were kin to the nightshade, used by witches to produce werewolves, and the German name for the fruit means "wolf peach." Linnaeus is the man who scientifically named the tomato Lycopersicon esculentum, *meaning "edible wolf peach."*

—Ozark superstitions

Asparagus helps promote elimination through urine. It is considered a liver tonic and contains amino acids.

If you have an abscessed tooth or a boil, apply a piece of onion to that area to draw out infection and encourage circulation for faster healing.

Eating fresh apples daily can help with gout and rheumatism.

Put a piece of fresh bread on a wound to stop bleeding

Apply vinegar to wasp stings to reduce swelling.

To cure warts, take a dead cat to a graveyard at midnight. When you hear a noise, throw the cat toward the sound—that will take the warts away. Or rub warts with a raw potato and bury the potato in clay.

To cure a cold, inhale the smoke of burning feathers.

To cure a stomachache, burn out an owl's nest on a mountain and then eat fruit out of it.

—Folklore remedies

CONTENTS

CONTENTS

CONTENTS

DEDICATION AND ACKNOWLEDGEMENTS

This book is dedicated to my uncle Richard Brantley and his chalkboard of words only an English teacher would know aimed in a verbal joust at a rowdy kid who is now writing books but is still without his command of the language.

To Project Vagabond, my "big sisters" in the belly dance community, who are always supportive.

To the gals of the group I'm part of, Gypsy Sol. I missed several classes while writing this book, and they have been so patient with me and concerned when I come to class looking tired from too many late nights at the keyboard. Thanks girls. I love you all. You are family and always offer encouragement when I need it.

To my kids: Jennifer, Charlene and Nathaniel. Charlene is part of my team, Route 66 Paranormal Alliance, and is a solid member. She's also helped with research for both my previous book, *Missouri's Haunted Route 66: Ghosts Along the Mother Road*, and this one. Nate experienced his first paranormal investigation with mom, and I think he's a natural; he's got a flair for the work.

To my grandchildren: Geoffrey, Madison, Tonia and Erica. Madison and Tonia have a tale they told me that I didn't have a spot for in the main text. They live just outside Warrenton, Missouri, on the northern edge of the Ozarks. Down the road from them is a small family plot, lost in obscurity. While I was visiting them in October 2010, the girls told me they had been to the graveyard and saw a dog walking among the tombstones. It disappeared in front of them, they said, and then reappeared before their eyes.

To Dean, my soul mate. What more can I say? He has to live with me while I'm off on lectures, out on investigations he can't make or up late at night writing. To Ali, Ken, Andrew and Jeanna, we wouldn't be a team without you.

A lot of people helped with this book. Photos came from Dave Harkins, Dean Pestana, Alicia Holder and Mark Dean. Stories came from Michael Greeley, Dave Harkins, Jeanna Barker, Brandi Osley, Kenneth Brewer, Tiffany Jussel, Darla Kelly, Jamey Leonard, Diane M. Henke and Jason Henke. Thanks to Steve Cottrell, for use of the information contained in his book *Haunted Ozark Battlefields*. Thank you to Nathaniel Wells, for letting Mom drag you along on one of her investigations and spending a chilly night before Halloween out roaming a foggy battlefield.

Thank you to the Route 66 Paranormal Alliance members—Alicia Holder, Kenneth Brewer, Jeanna Barker, Dean Pestana, Andrew Muller and Charlene Wells—for all the dedication they've shown in researching, gathering information to add to this book, taking photos and weathering the long nights of investigations to track down the stories of a haunting.

A big thank-you goes to my daughter, Jennifer, and my son-in-law, George (Bud) Burgmeyer, for allowing the paranormal team to bunk at their house in October 2010 as a base of operations while we attended the big-screen premiere of the Booth Brothers' *The Haunted Boy*. We were on overdrive investigating Zombie Road in the St. Louis area, doing book signings and investigating Enoch's Bridge, the Washington Brewery and cemeteries on what we came to call "Paranormal Hell Week."

INTRODUCTION

It's not that the mountains are so high, it's just that the valleys are so deep.
—Old folklore saying

Called the Ozarks Uplift or Ozarks Dome by geologists, the area covers about fifty or sixty thousand square miles of southern Missouri, northern Arkansas, eastern Oklahoma, southeastern Kansas and southwestern Illinois. The region is comparable to the size of Florida and is bordered by the Mississippi River on the eastern side, the Missouri River to the north, the Arkansas River to the south and the Great Plains, with the Osage and Neosho Rivers, to the west. In Missouri, the Ozarks blend into the Mingo Swamps at the Bootheel in the southeast.

Taum Sauk Mountain, west of Ironton, Missouri, is the tallest peak in the St. Francois Mountains at 1,772 feet. Arkansas' Boston Mountains have peaks as high as 2,000 feet.

The St. Francois Mountains are the core of the dissected uplift and bear the oldest rocks, formed by 440 million years of submergence beneath the ocean, uplift, erosions and deposits of limestone, granite, rhyolite and dolomite. The Ozarks and Ouachita Mountains together are known as the U.S. Interior Highlands.

Repeated stages of development for the Ozark region are the Cambrian Postosi Formation, the Eminence Formation, the Ordovician Gasconade Formation and the Roubidoux Formation. Each layer was separated by the moving of land plates, erosion and the addition of other materials—such as sandstone, shale and chert (flint)—that formed during stages of exposure. Sometime between seven million and fifty million years ago, the Tertiary uplift took place; this was the latest stage of erosion.

The sediments of sandstone, flint and shale are resistant to weathering, but dolomite and limestone dissolve in water. The years of lying beneath the seas and then being forced upward as the land moved have cause a pitted formation of land, much like a sponge with its many sinkholes, caves, streams and losing streams.

The topography is divided into four sections, mostly rolling hills and valleys. The sections are Springfield Plateau, Salem Plateau, St. Francois Mountains and the Boston Mountains. Divisions between the Springfield and Salem Plateaus are rugged, and the Boston Mountains have valleys ranging from 500 to 1,550 feet deep.

Unique Ozark geographical features are glades, grasses and forbs (herbaceous flowering plants) in shallow soil on exposed bedrock within otherwise heavily forested land, especially in Missouri. The land is rocky. Our yard in Springfield, Missouri, is rough for planting tomatoes, and digging out a garden can be frustrating at best.

Springfield is called a "Tree City" and showcases some of the glorious trees that make the Ozarks such a beautiful place to live.

Opinions differ on how the region got its name. Many think the word Ozarks is a derivation of the French term *Aux Arcs*, which translates to "Of the Bows." While as a kid I played with the green, cauliflower-like fruit called "hedge apples," the Osage Indians found a more practical use, constructing strong bows out of the wood of the Osage orange tree.

There are tales of the word Ozark coming from early people referring to rainbows, as in *aux arcs en ciel* "towards the rainbows." Another possibility is the French word for the bends, or arcs, in the Arkansas River. More derivations include "of the arches," in reference to the dozens of natural bridges formed by erosion and collapsed caves in the Ozark region. These include Clifty Hollow Natural Bridge (a series of arches) in Missouri and Alum Cove in the St. Francois National Forest.

Aux Arcs is also thought to be a shortened and corrupted French term meaning "to the Ozark Mountains" or, in the decades prior to the French and Indian War, "to (toward) Arkansas Trading Post." *Aux Arkansas* originally referred to the trading post at Arkansas Post located in wooded Arkansas Delta lowland above the confluence of the White River with the Mississippi River.

"Arkansas" appeared to be the French version of what the Illinois tribe (farther up the Mississippi) called the Quapaw, a tribe living in eastern

Arkansas in the area of the trading post. Eventually, the term came to refer to all Ozark Plateau drainage into the Arkansas and Missouri Rivers. In the twentieth century, "Ozarks" became a generic term for the region.

Plateau elevation ranges from 650 to 1640 feet above sea level. The rocks are Mississippian and Pennsylvanian carbonates, domed upwards, folded and faulted. Sixty-five million years ago, during the Tertiary period, water, lithology and erosion created the structural framework of the region, dissecting the land into rounded ridges cut through by narrow, steep-sided valleys. Rocks were dissolved by springs, sinkholes and caves, commonly called karst as a land feature.

The Ozark Plateau consists of about 70 percent forest, 20 percent pasture and 10 percent cropland. Soil consists of weathered carbonate rocks. Trees are mostly oak, pine and hickory.

Weather ranges from humid continental to humid subtropical, with precipitation between forty and fifty inches per year. The Ozark region, characterized by many underground streams and springs, is drained by the Osage, Gasconade, White and Black Rivers. Lake of the Ozarks, impounded by Bagnell Dam on the Osage River, provides power and recreation facilities. Taneycomo Lake, Bull Shoals Lake and Table Rock State Park are also recreation areas.

In Oklahoma, the Ozark Plateau covers a small portion of land, and the uplift in Kansas is even smaller. The Oklahoma Ozarks cover Cherokee, Adair (with portions of Ottawa), Delaware, Wagoner, Muskogee and Sequoyah Counties.

Nomadic hunter-gatherers inhabited the Ozark Plateau about fourteen thousand years ago. Archaeological digs have found remains in campsites and burial grounds. Pictographs give insight into the lives of these indigenous people. The Osage and Quapaw were not nomadic but lived in villages.

Jacques Marquette and Louis Joliet first explored the Ozarks about 1673 but did not enter present-day Oklahoma. White settlers, mostly French fur traders, are documented in the area about 1705. In 1770, the Spanish took possession. American settlers trickled in by 1790.

The Cherokee nation lived on the Oklahoma section of the Ozarks Plateau after it was removed from the South. Eight tribes occupied northwestern Oklahoma by 1890: the Cherokee, Seneca, Wyandotte, Ottawa, Quapaw, Peoria, Modoc and Shawnee.

ST. FRANCOIS MOUNTAINS

If you kill a toad, your cows will give bloody milk.
—Ozark superstition

Missouri boasts its own volcanic history in the location of the St. Francois Mountains, an outcrop of Precambrian igneous rock formed of spewed magma, hot gases and acid debris 250 million years ago. This fell and cooled, forming a dense layer of fine-grained igneous rhyolite over a heart of coarse-grained granite.

Shallow seas formed inland layering dolomite and sandstone, sediment upon sediment, several feet thick. The St. Francois Mountains (often misspelled St. Francis Mountains, matching local pronunciation) are one of the oldest exposures of rock in North America, with the Ozarks Dome elevations and stratigraphic inclines radiating downward from Taum Sauk's peak. This area is thought to be the only American Midwest region to have never been submerged, existing as an island archipelago in the Paleozoic seas. Even fossilized coral and the remains of reefs are found among the rock flanking the mountains.

The St. Francois Mountains are the center of the Missouri mining region, yielding iron, lead, barite, zinc, silver, manganese, cobalt, nickel ores and granite and limestone quarries. Potosi, Missouri, was considered the richest lead deposit in the world. Bell Mountain, near Potosi, is one of the tallest landforms in North America and part of the Missouri Wilderness. Part of the St. Francois Mountains, Bell has a twelve-mile trail ascending to its peak.

Historic Mine La Motte, near Fredericktown, saw lead mining activity by the French as early as 1720. An old granite quarry lies on the edge of Elephant Rocks State Park, a spectacular outcropping of huge, weathered, pinkish granite boulders set in a row like circus elephants on parade.

This range of mountains is said to contain some of the most unique natural features of the state of Missouri, with the most ancient landscapes and least-populated counties. Elephant Rocks, Johnson's Shut-Ins, the Black River and Sliver Mines and Devil's Tollgate are part of the attractions in the area.

Johnson's Shut-Ins lie pocketed away in the St. Francois Mountains among chutes, rivers, gorges and waterfalls. Plains cut out by the constant flow of water now host drought-hardy plants (normally found in the Southwest deserts) among the exposed rocks that share their space with the eastern collared lizard (which rises up to run on its back legs) and scorpions. There is a saying in the area: "Never put on your boots in the morning without shaking them out first."

Ancient peoples of America inhabited the Arcadia Valley at the end of the last ice age. They hunted big game, mastodon and the giant ground sloth. As the larger animals died off, the Indians adapted to hunting smaller game and to become forager-gatherers. Their arrowheads and spears became fluted for hunting; they made needles for sewing, nets for fishing and mortars for grinding seeds. Fish and vegetables became staples in their diet.

What is now Missouri once was home to the Hopewell Indians. They fired clay pots and tools, traded furs and built large ceremonial mounds. St. Louis once housed several of these mounds and was nicknamed the "Mound City." The largest of these mounds stood at what is now the intersection of Mound and Broadway Streets.

During the Mississipian period, the Native Americans depended more on the rivers and grew crops in the fertile riverbeds. Hernando de Soto and his men encountered the Indians in 1541 after crossing the Mississippi into Calpista and Palisema, modern-day Arcadia Valley and the Black River Recreation Area (this area includes Pilot Knob and Ironton and extends west to the Current River).

The last classified era of Native American development is the Historic period. Starting in 1700, the European explorers discovered tribes of Osage, Delaware, Kickapoo, Shawnee, Piankashaw and others.

It is thought that the Osage were the only Missouri-native tribe. The white man drove other Indians westward as they took over their lands across North America. The Osage were warlike and covered Missouri, Kansas, Oklahoma and Arkansas. Their numbers were greater than those of other tribes. Only the strongest males were allowed to marry and often gained the maiden of their choice, plus her sisters, implementing selective breeding that produced warriors over six feet tall.

A treaty with the Osage took from them most of their claim to the Ozark Plateau, but the Indians thought the treaty did not exclude them from hunting in the area. This often caused trouble with the white settlers, even though the Indians were mostly friendly and even traded and hunted alongside the white man. Various treaties relocated many tribes, and Native Americans became a rarity in the region after 1830. The Trail of Tears passes through the Ozarks, and the loss of many innocent lives haunts our soil. The first white settlers noted about twenty thousand Indians in Missouri.

One superior main street links two towns in the valley, Ironton and Arcadia. Small-town geniality and nineteenth-century buildings stand as a testimonial to the history of the Ozarks in this region. Ephraim Stout was the first white settler in the valley in 1805. On the banks of Stout's Creek, the first ironworks west of the Mississippi River were erected.

Arcadia Academy

Arcadia Valley Academy (1846) boasts some of the most beautiful architecture and stained-glass windows in the state. It is haunted by the Ursuline nuns who purchased the former Methodist high school and turned the building into a girls' school and convent. Some of the best citizens of southeast Missouri graduated from the school.

When the nuns first bought the property, only two of the original buildings existed. The sixteen-room school had only three rooms that were habitable. The unfinished four-story brick building built in 1870 also had three usable rooms.

For 150 years, the academy has towered over the valley. Built by Jerome C. Berryman, the building served as a Union hospital during the Civil War. After the nuns bought the academy, it operated as a school until 1970. When the nuns moved to St. Louis in 1985, the convent closed and is now under private ownership. Listed on the National Register of Historic Places as a historic district, the academy has two hundred rooms and forty-seven toilets. The gymnasium has a truss system designed in Germany, and the auditorium seats 250 people. The campus occupies seventeen acres and features nine buildings; only one building remains of the original campus, and it houses a bed-and-breakfast.

When run by the nuns, the girls' lives were strictly monitored; silence was to be maintained except during recreation.

Today, animals seem agitated at the site. Doors open in the night, and footsteps are heard in the halls, supposedly belonging to the nuns who ran the school. Children are often heard playing in the buildings. A Civil War soldier roams the location. A man buried in the cemetery on-site can be seen in the rooms or the hallway. Sounds of large objects being dragged over the floors are heard. Singing is reported. Doors locking and unlocking, odors, mists, the feeling of being touched and shadowy figures are all on the list of anomalies at the academy.

THE LEGEND OF MINA SAUK FALLS

Mina Sauk Falls in the Shut-Ins at Taum Sauk Mountain is the tallest waterfall in Missouri, and according to legend, the mountain's face displays the grief of Mina Sauk. She was the daughter of Sauk-Ton-Qua, called Taum Sauk by the white man and chief of the Piankishaw.

The Piankishaw tribe was smaller than the Osage, "the masters" of the area, and the Cherokee, but spent peaceful summers in the Arcadia Valley, "land of the flowers," hunting and raising corn. Limestone shelters along the bluffs of the Mississipi became their homes during the winter.

Mina's tale tells of her beauty and how men desired her. She met a young Osage warrior in the woods, and he wooed her in secret. The couple was discovered, and Mina's improper behavior cost the young man his life. He was executed on a porphyry outcropping of rock overlooking Taum Sauk Creek and facing Wildcat Mountain. Tossed off the mountain, he was speared by the warriors above when he landed on the succession of rock benches. At last, he lay dying in the valley below.

Mina, in her despair, fought her restraining tribesmen and broke free to leap from the peak, plunging over the cascade to the granite ledge two hundred feet below. This displeased the Great Spirit; the earth shook and trembled, and the rock broke away, revealing a stream of water rushing down to wash away the blood from the rock benches below.

The place where Mina lay became the origin of the name of the falls, and today small flowers with crimson petals bloom there, signifying the color of blood spilled that day.

Taum Sauk and its surrounding uplift neighbors are volcanic ancients, older many times over than the Appalachian Mountains. These mountains are part of the few areas never submerged by the seas. Glades—rocky, open expanses—dot the park, showing the scattered proof of volcanic birth and giving home to desert-adapted animals and plants such as Indian grass, little bluestem, rattlesnake master, ashy sunflower and white prairie clover.

Parlor Bed-and-Breakfast

Towns near the mountain claim their fair share of ghosts. Doorbells ring at both the front and back of the Parlor Bed-and-Breakfast in Ironton, Missouri. Clocks stop and then restart, radios turn off and on and motion-activated Christmas decorations become active when no one is near to set them into motion.

Snuggled in the Arcadia Valley, the Parlor invites guests to witness the antics of its disembodied tenants. The B&B is listed as having been a funeral parlor in a former life and is located near the haunted Fort Davidson Civil War battlefield, where the spirits of the soldiers who died there wander within sight of the ditch where their bodies were tossed. Also nearby is the equally haunted Pilot Knob Civil War Cemetery.

The Parlor is a lovely turn-of-the-century home built in 1908 by Charles J. Tual, noted architect of the late 1800s and early 1900s. The home was designed as a present for his bride and features stained-glass windows, turret rooms and private balconies.

A Mr. Howell bought the home in 1960 and operated a funeral parlor within its walls for a time. The current owner's grandfather's funeral was held there. The home was restored to its original state after being purchased by the current owners in 2000 and opened as the Parlor Bed-and-Breakfast.

Renovations seem to have awakened the old girl, as they do many older locations, although the B&B owners had been "warned" about the home. Voices were heard during the renovations. A shadowy female was spotted walking from the kitchen into the dining room. Apparitions stand at the foot of the guests' beds.

I often hear tales of people who buy a historic building with no knowledge of ghostly activity, only to have the spirits wake up once workmen enter and begin tearing into walls and foundations. When the front doorbell at the Parlor rings, it's without the batteries in place needed to make the doorbell operational. Warm and loving feelings are present here, unlike the heavy, oppressive "something" that many haunted locations share. People feel someone coming up behind them but no one is ever there.

A child has been seen jumping on the bottom of a bed in a room said to have belonged to a little girl. A phantom lady has been seen walking up the staircase that was walled off from the rest of the house. Clocks fall off the walls, curtains fly from the windows and objects disappear. Shadows are seen, a woman in a gray dress touches people, voices whisper and the temperature changes. Lights go off and on, and water is heard running in the bathroom when no one is present. Money disappears and reappears. A little boy watches people through a dining room window. Someone seems to play with a ball inside the house, bouncing it over the floor.

FORT DAVIDSON

A mere three hundred yards from the base of Pilot Knob Mountain, ghosts wander a battlefield, ready to continue their war. Confederate and Union soldiers have been seen on the ground where a rugged, but strategic, fort once stood. Missouri was a vital "border state" during the war, part of the Trans-Mississippi Theater, with over 600,000 square miles of prime land. The state was in many ways a wasteland in terms of the war, but it was also strategic for the flow of men and supplies. Control of St. Louis and the state was vital to both sides to give total access to the Mississippi River.

On September 27, 1864, Major General Sterling Price led a force of Confederate soldiers through Arcadia Valley in an attack on the earthen Fort Davidson as he moved through Ironton on his way to St. Louis.

Fort Davidson was a hexagonal fortress with walls nine feet high and ten feet thick. It was surrounded by a nine-foot-deep dry moat, with two long rifle pits running out from the walls. A reinforced board fence topped the thick wall. Entry was gained only by means of a drawbridge on the southeastern corner. To further the fort's protection, a cleared field extended in all directions beyond the walls, leaving any enemy exposed to guards keeping watch in the fort. The fort lay in a valley with large hills on three sides. In its center was a buried powder magazine. Artillery for the fort consisted of four thirty-two-pound siege guns, three twenty-four-pound howitzers and six three-inch ordnance rifles.

Price planned to seize the arsenal at St. Louis to boost the Confederate's campaign. He crossed from Arkansas into Missouri in September 1864 and moved north to Ironton near the southern terminus of the Iron Mountain Railroad.

With twelve thousand mounted infantry and three thousand unarmed men, the garrison of fifteen hundred men and seven guns at Pilot Knob was too tempting. Price received word that Union troops were heading south to intercept him and dispatched a detachment to destroy the railroad. He then focused his attention on capturing the fort.

Under Price, Major General John Sappington Marmaduke and Major General James Fagan drove their cavalry through Ironton Gap to defeat and capture Major James Wilson's Calvary between Pilot Knob and Sheppard Mountain. For Wilson's role in the December 25, 1863 massacre outside Doniphan, a Confederate military tribunal executed him and six of his troopers.

Wilson's troops had been ordered by Colonel R.G. Woodson to set free Union prisoners held at the town of Ponder. They rode out of Pilot Knob midmorning on the twenty-third for Doniphan, eighty miles to the south.

At 3:00 a.m. on December 25, Wilson's cavalry passed through Doniphan and continued west to Ponder, following the tracks of 150 horses in the winter mud of Missouri. They captured pickets as they went, preventing any warning for those gathered at the Pulliam Farm in southwestern Ripley County. On the farm, almost 150 officers and men of the Missouri State Guard's Fifteenth Cavalry Regiment, 102 Union prisoners, 60 civilians, many women and children and men of Company C, Missouri State Militia, met for a religious service led by Reverend Colonel Timothy Reeves. A Christmas dinner would follow for the reported 300 people at Pulliam's. More than a normal town gathering would be expected for a Christmas celebration.

Records indicate that the troops at Pulliam's had their arms stacked while they ate dinner when two companies of the Union Missouri State Militia, under Wilson's command, surprised them, shooting into the crowd and attacking with sabers. Over two hundred mounted cavalrymen rode into the farm, killing thirty Confederate men instantly and wounding several others. Reports said that most of the civilians were killed or wounded as well. Only the thirty-five men who guarded the prisoners on the farm were armed at the time Wilson's men descended.

The Union suffered no casualties, indicating that the Confederates did not have the chance to fire a single shot; 112 officers and men survived.

Bodies were taken to Doniphan for burial in the Old Doniphan Cemetery south of the courthouse. Tradition says that Negro men dug graves, and the town women wrapped the bodies for burial. Other bodies were buried where they fell in the Ponder and Union Grove Cemeteries.

That act has forever been known as Wilson's Massacre. The site of the bloody raid is called by many names: Battle Hollow, Battleground Hollow and Battlefield Hollow. Maps no longer show the location, but residents know where the incident took place.

After capture at Pilot Knob, Wilson and his men were stripped to the waist and marched barefoot behind Fagan's column to a farm ten miles west of Union and fifteen miles south of Washington, Missouri. Speculation has it that Wilson and his men were tried for murder and shot on October 24, 1864, by a firing squad composed of men from the Fifteenth Missouri Cavalry Regiment.

Other accounts claim that in September 1864, Major James Wilson, along with six of his men captured by the Confederates, was held for one week before being turned over to Major Tim Reeves, CSA (a guerrilla by Union standards) under Marmaduke's command. Wilson was taken out and hanged, and the other men were shot.

General Rosecrans received word of this murder and issued an order to retaliate. Rosecrans was commander of the Department of the Missouri Military Cavalry, and his order stated that a Rebel major and six enlisted men were to be shot. Only prisoners who refused to take an oath of allegiance to the Federal government were selected. Those prisoners were marched into a room with the orders to draw lots from a container held above eye level so they couldn't see within. Marbles of black or white were inside the container; those who drew the white were spared, and those who drew one of the six black marbles were executed.

The Battle of Pilot Knob began with Price's leading forces encountering Union pickets south of Ironton, three miles south of Fort Davidson.

During the battle, the Federal troops were driven back into town with exchange of gunfire on the Iron County Courthouse lawn. Damage from stray bullets still dots the building's structure.

Price assaulted the fort from many sides. A brigade went over the top of Pilot Knob to encounter a small Union force; another mounted the summit of Shepherd's Mountain. A third rounded Shepherd's Mountain to the northeastern side of the fort, and the fourth snaked through a valley between the mountains.

Union forces were driven back, severely outnumbered, and the Confederates took Shepherd's Mountain. A two-gun battery was deployed, and subsequent fire on the fort forced the smaller of the rifle pits to be abandoned.

The attacks did not come simultaneously, an error on Price's part, allowing the fort's cannons to focus on each Confederate unit in turn.

Fagan's men met staggering gunfire from the fort and broke for the rear, except for William Cabell's brigade, which fought its way into the moat

ORDER No. 11

At sunrise, August 21, 1863, William Quantrill led about 400 men into Lawrence, Kansas, seeking revenge on those who had wreaked havoc on Missouri for years. The guerillas burned over 180 buildings and killed over 150 men and boys. After the attack, they were pursued by Union troops back to Cass County, Missouri, where they disbanded and disappeared into the brush.

Four days later, August 25, 1863, Brigadier General Thomas Ewing, Union Commander of the District of the Border, issued General Orders No. 11. This district included the border counties of Jackson, Cass, Bates, and northern Vernon. Ewing's order mandated the evacuation of the district's civilian population regardless of loyalty, with the exception of a few specifically identified towns which became military stations: Kansas City, Independence, Hickman Mills, Pleasant Hill, and Harrisonville.

The objective of this extreme measure was to discourage a retaliatory attack by Kansans and to prevent more raids and killing by bushwhackers. It attempted to eliminate the food, water, and shelter for Southern sympathizers and guerillas. Grain and hay were confiscated or burned in the field as were all structures outside of the military stations.

Ewing's order allowed only 15 days for complete evacuation. Everyone quickly had to seek safe haven. With most men away fighting, women and children sorted possessions. Sometimes they hid or buried valuables for future reclamation. Limited clothing and food were packed while everything else was left behind.

Refugees unable to prove their Union loyalty, and thus denied shelter in the five military stations, began their exodus under a sweltering sun, while walking in clouds of dust. Roads soon filled largely with women, children, and the elderly. Most healthy horses, usable wagons, and buggies had long since been taken by either Union troops or bushwhackers.

As a result, people walked out of the border counties, many barefoot, carrying their few possessions. A fortunate few had wagons or make-shift carts pulled by small oxen, broken-down plow horses, milk cows, or animals purposely blinded to make them unfit for the guerrillas or military.

ORDER No.11
"All persons..are hereby ordered to remove from their present places of residence within fifteen days"

Brig. General Thomas Ewing

General Order No. 11 resulted in the "Burnt District." *Photo by Janice Tremeear.*

surrounding Fort Davidson. Wood-finned impact grenades thrown by the Union forces inside the fort pinned down Cabells's men. Unable to scale the earthen walls, the Confederates fell back.

General Thomas Ewing (General William T. Sherman's brother-in-law), in command of the fort, repeatedly denied surrender. Within Fort Davidson were African American civilians, and Ewing, fearful of a slaughter similar to the slaying of black soldiers earlier in the year at Fort Pillow, Tennessee, refused to give in to Price's demands.

Ewing was also concerned for his own safety if he surrendered. He was responsible for General Order No. 11, which had resulted in an eviction notice sent to all people in the area of Jackson, Cass, Bates and Vernon Counties in western Missouri, who could not prove their loyalty to the Union cause. This order became a virtual "license to kill" and left many families without husbands or sons.

This area today is known as the "Burnt District," as Ewing's decree virtually wiped out the entire region at the time of the Civil War. The population of Cass County dropped from ten thousand to six hundred.

Union troops held Fort Davidson until dusk. Under the cover of darkness, General Ewing ordered his men out of the fort to rendezvous with troops in St. Louis. Ewing had his men muffle the hooves of their horses with burlap, drape the drawbridge with canvas and evacuate. They decamped on the road to Caledonia after midnight.

Behind them, they left a slow-burning fuse in the powder magazine. The explosion that resulted left a large hole in the fort. Today, the hole remains and is now a round pond. Price didn't investigate until the next day; this pause lost him the campaign. The dead scattered the field—seventy-five Union soldiers and hundreds of Confederate soldiers. The bodies were buried in one of the trenches surrounding the fort, unmarked and unknown.

Ulysses S. Grant received the rank of brigadier general at Ironton in 1861, and both the courthouse and the gazebo on the lawn are listed on the National Register of Historic Places. Visitors to the monument at Pilot Knob have reported witnessing the appearance of soldiers and cannons on the field, only to watch them disappear when approached.

CALEDONIA WINE COTTAGE

During the Battle of Pilot Knob, the wounded from both sides were treated in a makeshift hospital in Caledonia. That building became what is now the Caledonia Wine Cottage. Diseased soldiers were quarantined in a locked bedroom on the third floor. A hole was cut into the padlocked door to pass through food and water; it remains to this day within the Wine Cottage. Confederate soldiers were held prisoner in the basement, and the windows still have the bars from that time.

Nestled in the woodlands of the St. Francois Plateau, the 185-year-old house witnessed the tragedy of the Cherokee who passed by on the Trails of Tears and the atrocities of the Civil War. A young girl was killed curbside as a passing vehicle hit her.

Jacob Fisher bought lot 18 in the newly formed town of Caledonia, Missouri, in 1824. The Stage Stop Inn began life via slave labor. The three-story, twelve-room house with a dirt-floor basement hid three tunnels. Two tunnels led to houses on either side of the main building; the third led to a nearby creek. A separate door at the back of the house allowed the slaves to enter apart from the owners and to make use of the tunnels to move between workplaces.

The Underground Railroad utilized these tunnels later; they are now filled in. The home boasts a continuous three-story walnut staircase (the only kind in the Ozarks, it is said) and the oldest persimmon tree in the state.

Jacob brutally beat a female slave to death in 1829. Her name was Patience. She suffered before she died with broken arms, a slash above her right eye, a smashed and cut ear, bruising and, finally, a broken neck. Jacob fled in January of that same year after the murder. His property was sold, and rumors suggested he was living in Mississippi.

At the north edge of Caledonia, a marker denotes the place where sixteen thousand Cherokee trod to a new territory in November 1837 after being forced off their native soil. After nine hundred miles of marching, four thousand did not live to see the trail's end.

In the later part of the twentieth century, the Ramseys owned the house. William Ramsey passed away inside the house in 1976 as he rested on the couch. His widow, Hallie (Haley in some accounts), spent her remaining days tending her garden and watching the traffic from the second-story balcony. She died in August 1993 while resting in her favorite chair.

After a brief stint as an antique shop, the building now serves as a restaurant, bed-and-breakfast and wine shop. The building is listed on the National Register of Historic Places.

Other odd bits of history within the building include voices sounding in empty halls, sightings of a shadowy Civil War soldier and footsteps echoing throughout the house. One of the stranger reports is of corks popping out of noncarbonated wine bottles. Animals watch empty rooms, wary to enter. Objects are thrown or dropped, and wall hangings are found lying on the floor. Children wave at people unseen by adults. A man in a hat is seen at various times of the day.

GAD'S HILL ROBBERY

This is a tale concerning Mr. Jesse Woodson James, one of many such legendary yarns spun about the man in the state of Missouri.

One hot and muggy summer night, Jesse and Frank James stole a stagecoach near Pilot Knob and pulled it across the railroad tracks, blocking the Iron Mountain Railroad. When the engineer saw the blockade, he locked up the brakes and pulled on the train whistle as it ground slowly to a screeching halt. Jesse was so annoyed by the train's racket of grinding wheels and screaming whistle that, enraged, he shot the engineer in the face.

Now the ghost of the engineer haunts the area near the tracks of the Iron Mountain Railroad, seeking revenge on those who dare come close to the tracks at night. Hot summer nights in Arcadia Valley will suddenly get quiet, with no sound of crickets. This is the signal. You may hear the rumble of the oncoming train and the wailing, mournful call of the whistle as it draws closer and closer. If you hear this sound, the engineer is coming for you.

Tales like this were told about Jesse James around campfires for years. The truth of the story is close, but without the ghost.

January 31, 1874, was not a hot summer night, but it's the date when Jesse and Frank, with between five and eight members of the James-Younger Gang, waited for the train at Gad's Hill (in some accounts, known as Gad's Lull) about thirty miles south of Pilot Knob.

This small settlement contained three houses, a store/post office and the small railroad platform, and was considered of no account. Only about fifteen people occupied the Ozark village. Normally, the train stopped just to exchange mailbags.

On this day, the southbound Little Rock Express had been scheduled to stop for a passenger, state representative L.M. Farris of Reynolds County. His sixteen-year-old son, Billy, arrived by wagon to meet him and waited at the store, where other men dropped in to chat with storekeeper Tom Fitz.

Reports say that five armed gunmen rode in from the southeast, hats low over their foreheads and faces hidden by white hooded masks bearing triangular cuts for eyeholes. The gang had tied up several men the night before, after spotting them walking on the train platform. They then placed a flag in the middle of the tracks.

After rousting the townspeople and robbing the storekeeper of $700 to $800, they forced the townspeople to help them build and set ablaze a bonfire on the tracks to catch the train conductor's attention when the train came by later that day. Conductor C.A. Alford stopped the train about 4:45 p.m. when it came toward the depot.

Alford got out of the train to investigate the fire but was captured by the gang. Ferris avoided being robbed after his son gave him a warning, and he stepped off the train to join the villagers.

Two gang members boarded the train and dragged the engineer, William Wetton; fireman A. Cambell; and brakeman Ben van Stumit off the train. Passengers were warned to stay aboard the train by another gang member riding alongside, shooting his gun.

Other members boarded the train to loot the safe. As a joke, one of the gang members took express agent Bill Wilson's receipt book and wrote inside: "Robbed at Gad's Hill."

Once the safe was empty, the gang strode through the passenger car. Any man who had the well-groomed, uncalloused hands of a wealthy man was robbed of money and jewelry. Stories tell of the masked men's lighthearted behavior; they patted the heads of children they passed in the passenger car and bowed politely to the ladies. One exchanged his battered hat for a well-dressed man's fine hat.

A man suspected of being a Pinkerton agent was strip-searched, but no weapon was found on him. John F. Lincoln and John L. Merriam, two bankers, were taken off the train and forced to strip down to their underwear as the robbers laughed and took all their belongings.

When the robbers mounted their horses and rode off, one of them tossed a note to engineer Watton. This was assumed to be Jesse James giving out a note written by his own hand. One newspaper article reported:

> *The most daring robbery on record. The southbound train on the Iron Mountain Railroad was robbed this evening by five heavily armed men and robbed of ------ dollars. The robbers arrived at the station a few minutes before the arrival of the train, and arrested the Agent, put him under guard, and then threw the train on the switch. The robbers are all large men, none of them under six feet tall. They were all masked and started in a southerly direction after they robbed the train, all mounted on fine-blooded horses. There is a hell of excitement in this part of the country.*

The gang members considered themselves invincible. Later, the James-Younger Gang killed Pinkerton agent Joseph Whicher. Also after this robbery, Jim and John Younger were involved in a gunfight with three Pinkerton agents. Two of those men, Louis J. Lull and Ediwn B. Daniels, were killed.

The gang got away with between $10,000 and $12,000 from the train at Gad's Hill (other stories say the amount was $8,000; some say $22,000). Present in the gang were Jesse and Frank James and Cole, John and Bob Younger. It is possible that Clell Miller, Arthur McCoy and Jim Reed also partook in the robbery.

The first railroad company to build in southeast Missouri was the St. Louis Iron Mountain and Southern Railroad Corporation in 1851 by a special act of the Missouri legislature. The railroad existed to make the iron ore around Iron Mountain, Missouri, available to the river and other areas. This line ran from St. Louis to Pilot Knob and extended later into Bollinger County and connected at Allenville. Later acquired by the Missouri Pacific Line (Union Pacific), it was abandoned in 1984.

A group of investors bought a steam-powered train with coaches of 1920 vintage to operate as a tourist attraction on four acres formerly known as the Loos Saw Mill. One of the events for the train is a mock robbery by the James-Younger Gang.

SALEM PLATEAU

To keep the devil away, throw salt over your left shoulder.
—Ozark superstition

The bulk of the Ozarks exist within the Salem Plateau. It is estimated that the last time the earth lifted and dropped beneath the sea was fifty million years ago. Geologists call the region the Ozark peneplane. Lowland surrounds the Ozarks on all sides. At the Missouri Bootheel, the Mingo swamps spread from the foothills to the bottom corner of the state. The plateau occupies the midsection of Missouri from just north of the Missouri River to the Arkansas border. Forty-nine counties are in the Salem Plateau, and the region wraps around the St. Francois Mountains. Entry into this area via Interstate 44 can take one on a scenic tour. Within this area lie the Meramac River, Mark Twain State Park, the Irish Wilderness and the White River Trace where the Cherokee marched on the Trail of Tears.

Flora and fauna in the Ozarks can be as mysterious as the tales of ghosts and witches. Red fern is a thing of myth belonging on the lists of cyptozoology. It may not fit into the realm of a true fern, but try to tell an Ozarker that the pretty, frilly plant doesn't exist. The bract (leaf structure) isn't correct for a fern, yet legends have sprung around the plant and inspired a book, *Where the Red Fern Grows* (Bantam Books, 1961) by Wilson Rawls.

Among the cryptids of Missouri are the thunderbird, reported sailing the skies near Eureka. The Ozark howler, or Ozark black howler, is a black panther of legendary size. Several witnesses have spotted panthers in the state, but

The Ozarks, sunset through a barn. *Postcard courtesy Janice Tremeear.*

whether the giant mammal of the howler status exists remains to be proven. MoMo the Monster was Missouri's version of Bigfoot. It appears he was the brainchild of children playing pranks in the city of Louisiana, Missouri, but that doesn't explain the various sightings of a Bigfoot-type creature in Missouri and Arkansas. Other Bigfoot-type creatures are the Bearman Monster near Sedalia, Missouri, and "Red Eyes" around Sullivan, Missouri. Reports of a Bigfoot-type creature date back to the Native Americans.

Werewolves have been reported, and the famous Nixa Hellhound was tracked south of Springfield, Missouri. I've read accounts of giant piranha sighted at the Lake of the Ozarks, but we know how fishermen like to exaggerate don't we? However, it is widely reported that giant catfish live next to Bagnell Dam—fish large enough to suck a full-grown man into their mouths, large enough to frighten experienced divers.

Centipedes of abnormal size are said to slither through the Ozark woodlands. Those of seven inches in length have been recorded, with tales of even longer creatures existing. The flying "rods" are everywhere— those elongated, swirling objects with "wings" along their sides, the "ghost centipedes" of the air.

Missouri is a state of contradictions: large cities with the wealth and crime to rival more notable coastal cities, institutions in smaller towns that train scientists and locales still very remote and mystery-ridden. Sprinkled liberally throughout the state are (or have been) places bearing names of wonder: Pumpkin Center, Devil's Elbow (twelfth on Realtor. com's 2009 list of the "50 Scariest City Names") and Lance—all names associated with Halloween.

The town of Frankenstein, Missouri, has a population of thirty and is the only town so named in the United States.

Towns with a Valentines theme for names include Romance, Love Lake and Orchid. Then there are the Christmas- or holiday-named towns of Noel, Jolly, Snow, Reindeer, Comet, Pilgrim and Star.

We Missourians have places named Zebra, Cooter, Enough, Licking, Peculiar, Roach, Sleeper, Knob Lick, Racket and Bland, and there's even a Climax Springs and Conception, Missouri.

Tightwad, Missouri, owes its place name to the plight of a poor mailman who bought a sixty-pound watermelon for $1.50 from a local shopkeeper. The mailman left the watermelon in the store to finish his route for the day. In his absence, another patron offered to buy the same watermelon for $2.00. The storekeeper, not thinking his actions were wrong, sold the watermelon to the second man, even though the postman had already paid it for. When the mailman returned for his watermelon, he was angry to say the least. The storeowner refused to refund the mailman's money. The mailman left the store calling the owner "Tightwad," and the name stuck.

Wood-Smith Castle

Missouri has several castles or castlelike structures. Some are public buildings, some are private homes and others are skeletal remains of someone's dream. Pythian Castle in Springfield has a long history and ghosts keeping the place busy. Pythian's story is written in my book *Missouri's Haunted Route 66: Ghosts Along the Mother Road.*

Wyeth-Tootle Castle and Barbosa's Castillo are in St. Joseph. Barbosa's is a wonderful restaurant with some amazing Mexican food. I've eaten there while on a trip to conduct a paranormal investigation of the Glore Psychiatric Museum. Barbosa's original name is Moss Castle; townspeople said that in 1891, at the address of 906 Sylvanie, there sat "a fabled castle of fantastic medievalism."

Old Cross Castle (Little Castle) is being built at the Lake of the Ozarks about ten miles from the Ha Ha Tonka Castle.

Stuart Castle is in Eureka.

Located at 5200 Cherry Street on the campus of the University of Missouri–Kansas City is the Epperson House Castle. Epperson Castle was built in 1923 by millionaire banker Uriah Epperson and donated to the university in 1942. Reportedly, Epperson Castle is one of the top five haunted houses in the United States.

Webb Castle in Independence sat across from the Mount Washington Cemetery with legends of ghosts that doom those who disturbed them. Sadly, the castle is now gone.

Bothwell Lodge–Sedalia's Castle is on the Hill in Sedalia.

Vaile Mansion is a castlelike home in Independence, Missouri.

Rockcliffe Mansion is another castlelike structure in Hannibal, Missouri. Rockcliffe is the home of Ken and Lisa Marks, who give ghost tours and have written a book for The History Press entitled *Haunted Hannibal*. They include their home's story in their book. I've met Ken and Lisa; they have fascinating tales and legends about the ghosts and haunts in the city of Hannibal.

Sky High Castle near Joplin is viewed from the town of Reddings Mill, sitting below the castle and the solid chert cliffs.

The Jackson County Jail Castle was built as a prison in 1897 and is located at 2001 Pine Street in Kansas City, Missouri.

Located right in the town square in Carthage is the magnificent castlelike Jasper County Courthouse building. Built from 1894 to 1895, the Jasper County Courthouse has turrets, arches and towers and was built to resemble a castle in the Romanesque Revival architectural style.

The castlelike Kansas City Museum, known as Corinthian Hall, is a twenty-five-thousand-square-foot mansion built by millionaire lumber baron Robert A. Long in the Beaux Arts architectural style in 1908. It was the Long family's home until 1939, when they donated Corinthian Hall to the Kansas City Museum Association.

De Soto has an unnamed castle, supposedly one of a pair that a wealthy St. Louisan planned to build to conduct mock battles between the two. The first was never completed after the man's wife died, and the second was never begun. The castle served as a nursing home.

Kansas City has the Wallace House Castle, Tiffany Castle and the City Workhouse Castle.

Festus has the Kennett's Castle, known as Selma Hall. It served as a fort during the Civil War.

A home in St. Louis, privately owned, is called the Castle of Montebello and has several castlelike features.

East of St. Clair on Iron Hill Road stands a creation that resembles a sprawling castle compound.

Cuba has Rock Castle.

A four-story castle tower, complete with a cannon on top, stands next to a home in Northmoor outside Kansas City.

Ha Ha Tonka Castle will be covered later in this book.

Another ruin of what was once planned as a building of marvelous stature is in Bee Tree Park, near St. Louis: the Wood-Smith Castle.

George F. Wood-Smith emigrated from Scotland in the early 1900s. With his fortune in hand, he planned a Scottish castle on a bluff overlooking the Mississippi River in south St. Louis County. George was a mere twenty years old when he set foot in North America. He would become a millionaire more than once during his lifetime, but he died broke. He was an inventor, a friend of Henry Ford and a Sunday dinner guest of Thomas Edison.

Born of a Glasgow doctor in 1880, George earned a degree in marine engineering at the University of Edinburgh in Scotland. He was a shipbuilder on the East Coast in America and an engineer for the Pennslyvania Railroad. He designed tank cars and railroad switches and then got into the oil business as America became infatuated with the automobile. Unfortunately, George never took out any patents on his designs.

In 1914, he began building his castle south of St. Louis on 420 acres of land at the end of Fine Road. It was a mock version of the castle near Glasgow where his aunt, Lady Jane Maxwell, lived. He planned it as a chateau from the King Louis XIII period and commissioned Raymond E. Maritz Sr. as the architect. Laclede's Landing still holds on file the eighty-six-year-old blueprints with the Missouri Historical Society.

Twenty rooms were planned, along with eleven bathrooms, a dining room overlooking the Mississippi River, two swimming pools (one outdoor, one indoor), a billiard room, servants' quarters, guest rooms, sunken gardens, a tower, a waterfall fountain, tennis courts, a golf course and a stable.

Most workers of the period earned $13 a week, and George hired a small army, spending $1,000 a week on building his dream. In 1920, his fortune changed. The sunken gardens were built, as were the towers and a magnificent stone staircase. The remaining construction sputtered along until the stock market crashed in 1929.

Thirty-foot walls stand with the sunken stone pool and gardens. A staircase with fifteen steps leading up to the first landing and another thirty leading up to the castle wall keeps vigil with the outside walls.

Pieces of the crumbling castle are legendary ornaments in front yards of homes in south St. Louis County.

The ruins are haunted with tales similar to other abandoned locations. One tale says that the castle remained unfinished because George's young son fell to his death while playing on-site. Another tale says George became enamoured of a younger woman. One story says his wife left him for another man.

A tragedy did strike the family when George's daughter, Sylvia, fell into a cistern and drowned.

The Wood-Smiths were said to have lived a life akin to the Great Gatsby. The *Goldenrod Showboat* often stopped at the boat landing on the Mississippi where George had a thirteen-room house on the grounds of the present-day Sherwood Country Club. He added a nine-hole golf course for his friends at the location.

After the stock market crash, George moved on to other things. The Ford Motors Company bought his castle but the planned assembly plant was never built, and Union Electric bought the land in 1948. The property is now fenced off with a Keep Out sign.

George earned a teacher's certificate at the University of Missouri in Columbia and at age sixty-eight became a vocational instructor in a boys' home in Boise, Idaho. George died in 1961 at age eighty-one.

JEFFERSON COUNTY

Paint the doors of your house red to prevent spirits from entering.
—Irish tradition

KIMMSWICK

Reports of a haunted graveyard on Montebello Camp Road exist here in the Ozark foothills. Theodore Kimm, the town's founder, is buried at this site, along with his wife and child. Chills and uneasy feelings are present, along with a glowing fog that rises from the oldest grave.

Kimmswick Bridge is home to balls of light.

Then there's the Old House (1770), the largest and most historical log building relocated to Kimmswick. Originally, it was on Highway 61/67 in the part of Arnold, Missouri, known as Beck. It was a dogtrot—two buildings united by a roof connecting the two—and was said to date from Revolutionary times.

A second story and a back two-story log wing were added in 1831. It served as an overnight stop for travelers and then later as a tavern. Some say that General U.S. Grant came here when he was stationed at Jefferson Barracks.

The house was taken down in two weeks in 1973; however, the reconstruction stretched over five years. Today it is called the Old House Steak House. Located on 6035 Second Street, at the corner of Second and

Elm Streets, it houses three ghosts: a little girl and boy and the ghost of an adult man called Amos. Reports claim that the apparitions have been seen inside the restaurant.

Theodore Kimm moved from St. Louis into Jefferson County in 1850 with his purchase of a large tract of land located where Little Rock Creek flows into the Mississippi. Humans have occupied that area since the ice age; the Clovis culture Indians hunted mastodons and other prehistoric animals in the swampy land. Mineral springs evaporated, leaving salt, and the white man was attracted to the location.

The French owned the land first but lost their claim during the French and Indian War. Spain then took hold of the land west of the Mississippi until 1800, when Napoleon Bonaparte signed a secret treaty with Spain giving him control. He sold the land three years later to the United States while Thomas Jefferson was president.

The Spanish used the same inland trail that animals and the Indians followed to make their way upriver from New Madrid to St. Louis. The trail was named El Camino Real and passed near what would become the city of Kimmswick. The Real is the oldest road in Missouri and is marked with a red granite boulder placed in 1917 by the Missouri Daughters of the American Revolution. To the French, this road was known as Rue Royale.

Captain George Washington Waters served at Jefferson Barracks just outside of St. Louis and was appointed surveyor for Jefferson County. He bought the land that the Waters family later sold to Theodore Kimm.

In 1854, the St. Louis and Iron Mountain Railroad was built along the Mississippi River, uniting St. Louis and Pilot Knob. An influx of traders and farmers in 1858 prompted Kimm to lay out a grid work pattern for the town he was building, a town named after himself. "Wick" means town or village, or even "salt spring" or "brine pit." It's possible that Theodore knew Thomas Jones had established a saltworks in the area before 1779, losing his efforts to the raids of hostile Indians seventy years before Kimm owned the land. In naming the town, he referred to his native city of Brunswick, Germany, combining his name with the city's.

Kimm sold vacant lots divided by alleyways. He built some homes and sold them on deeds of trust to encourage tradesmen to settle in Kimmswick.

Growth took hold, and by 1867 the town had a brewery, a steam flour mill, a brickyard, a copper shop, a wagon maker, a blacksmith shop, a saloon, mercantile stores, a lumberyard, a slaughterhouse, butcher shops, a bootery, a barbershop, a jeweler, a drugstore, a post office, an iron forge, a limestone quarry, greenhouses, doctors and three schools. One of the doctors' homes carries the rumors of haunting to this day from failed medical procedures performed on-site.

Mr. Kimm was postmaster and also gave an acre of ground to the city for a cemetery. Fresh flowers and spring water were shipped to St. Louis. By 1976, Kimmswick was the second largest city in Jefferson County.

After he retired in 1872, Mr. Kimm and his wife traveled in Europe. He offered the remainder of his lands for sale and dedicated a section at the corner of Third and Market Streets as the public marketplace. He also set aside a block to become the public park, known as Jefferson Square.

Theodore's wife died in St. Louis in 1876. She was buried next to their only child, Ernest Peltzer-Kimm, who died in 1853 at age nine. Mr. Kimm crossed the Atlantic Ocean twenty-nine times before his death in Switzerland on February 5, 1886.

KIMMSWICK BONE BED

Something rare in North America exists near Kimmswick, Missouri. Mineral springs made swampy conditions with mineral-rich mud. Mammals became bogged down and trapped and are preserved in the mud for all time, hardened into stone.

The second discovery of a mastodon kill site came in 1979. Clovis points were proven to be in direct association with the bones of a mastodon.

About 417 feet above sea level, Mastodon State Historic Site is an archaeological and paleontological site in Imperial, Missouri, about twenty miles south of St. Louis, on a sixty-five-foot limestone-terraced bluff containing the Kimmswick Bone Bed. The area is at the confluence of the Rock and Black Creeks, approximately one mile from the Mississippi River.

Bones of mastodons and other extinct animals were first found here in the early 1800s. The area gained fame as one of the most extensive Pleistocene ice age deposits in the country and attracted scientific interest worldwide.

History was made when scientists excavated a stone spear point made by hunters of the Clovis culture (ten to fourteen thousand years ago). This was the first solid evidence of the coexistence of people and these giant prehistoric mammals, which would have provided a supply of raw materials for clothing and food.

Today, the 425-acre preserve is on the National Register of Historic Places. A museum, a full-sized replica of a mastodon skeleton, a picnic area, several trails and a special-use campground offer visitors the chance to explore the cultural story of the oldest American Indians.

WAYNE COUNTY

Tales surrounding scorpions are handed down from the Egyptians, who
believed the arachnids came from the corpses of crocodiles. They also harbored
the idea that women were immune to the sting of a scorpion. Even the English
felt that bruising sweet bay leaves would breed scorpions. Some think the sting
is deadly only in the morning, and Ozark superstition says if surrounded by
fire, a scorpion will sting itself to death.
—Myths and folklore

LEEPER MANSION

Brandi Ousley, a friend who lives near Chillicothe, Missouri, offers the
following tale of Leeper Mansion:

> *Leeper Mansion has a very morbid history. Captain Leeper, who was*
> *a carpetbagger in the Civil War times, used to beat, shoot and hang the*
> *African Americans or just people he didn't like who came in on the new*
> *railroad being built. When he was on his deathbed, he was tied down*
> *because he kept yelling that demons were trying to get him. He was buried*
> *in his backyard in the family cemetery. At night, he has been seen walking*
> *up Leeper Holler, and there have been several reports of lights coming on*
> *and off, doors being shut and strange noises coming from his old bedroom.*

This is where you hear screams at night and doors slam shut; windows will be opened that were closed, etc. It is haunted not just by Captain Leeper but by several prostitutes that were savagely killed in the house. It has been vacant for many years (at least forty-five). A family redid it, and now they will not stay due to the nightly haunts.

W.T. Leeper was born William Thomas Leeper in Kentucky and bought 225 acres in Wayne County in 1857 where present-day Leeper and Mill Spring now stands. Opposed to the Confederates, he founded Company D of the Twelfth Regiment of Missouri Militia and became captain.

He became wild, taking a band of his men "hunting" for Southern sympathizers and killing unarmed men in the process. On February 4, 1863, Leeper and the Twelfth ambushed Daniel McGee and twenty-eight other people at the home of Simeon Cato.

During 1864, many Confederates deserted their units to return home and protect their families. Daniel McGee was one of these men, leading a group of local ex-soldiers in guerrilla warfare against the Union militia to stop harassment and hostilities toward their families.

McGee's group of men attacked Union troops of Company K, Sixty-eighth Enrolled Missouri Militia, under First Lieutenant James T. Sutton at Bollinger's Mill on February 4 at 12:40 a.m. The skirmish was short, and four Union soldiers were taken prisoner. The party separated, and McGee rode to the farm of his uncle.

The "McGee Massacre" (also referred to as the "Mingo Swamp Massacre") occurred when Leeper and his men descended on the farm. Many of McGee's men were unarmed, and the number of arms and horses Leeper reported taken from the farm was less than the number of men killed. Several men were elderly members of the Cato family; one was supposedly Richard Cato, the seventy-eight-year-old great uncle of Daniel McGee. They are reported as having been seated at the time of the raid and unarmed. Leeper gave the "no prisoners" order, and all twenty-nine people were killed. Daniel McGee was shot so many times that his torso was nearly severed in two.

Leeper convinced the Iron Mountain Railroad to run through his property, even though this meant they had to cut into two mountains. The Clarkson Sawmill moved to Leeper in 1872 and, combined with the railroad, spurred a "boomtown." The town was officially founded in 1874. Called Leeper Station, the town had a post office, a hotel and four stores. Ozark Hotel in Leeper was considered one of the most elaborate Wayne County resorts in the early twentieth century.

FRANKLIN COUNTY

Feed a cat out of an old shoe, and your wedding day will be a happy one.

*If a cat sneezes in front of a bride on the day before her wedding,
it is a sign of very good luck.*

It is a sign of very good luck to find a spider crawling on your wedding gown.

*Other good omens: seeing a rainbow, having the sun shine,
meeting a black cat, meeting a chimney sweep.*

—Wedding superstitions

Moving west, one of the largest counties was established two years before Missouri was admitted into the Union. Organized in 1818, Franklin County was once part of St. Louis County. At the time, only five counties existed in the Missouri Territory: St. Charles, St. Louis, Ste. Genevieve, Cape Girardeau and New Madrid. The years between 1812 and 1820 saw these five counties increase into fifteen, with Washington, Howard, Jefferson, Franklin, Wayne, Lincoln, Madison, Montgomery, Pike and Cooper added.

While there is a county named Washington, it is near metro St. Louis, and the city of Washington sits in the middle of Franklin County (named for Benjamin Franklin). The town of Newport was first selected as county seat until the state legislature removed it to Union.

Franklin was a wild land, covered with peavine, brush, rush and buffalo grass and a home to rattlesnakes, copperheads, spreadheads and all types of venomous creatures. Hardy settlers claimed and established hamlets along the Missouri River and carved out ports and landings along the major trade route. The Missouri River is the longest river in the Untied States at over 2,340 miles. Named after the Missouri Indians, it's the second largest tributary of the Mississippi River.

WASHINGTON

West of the Mississippi was a vast rolling land claimed for France by La Salle, who named it Louisiana in honor of the king. Changing hands to Spain and then back to France, the country was finally purchased by the United States in 1803. Soldiers and priests from France explored the region early on; trading posts were established in St. Louis and St. Charles, and hunters and trappers made their mark deep in the woods of what is now Missouri.

Established villages sprang up along the Missouri River and still bear French names, such as Femme Osage, Du Bois, Bourbeuse and Boeuf. As land grants became available, settlers began their journey up the Missouri River on keelboats and flatboats and alongside the river on horseback or on foot.

Daniel Boone accelerated travel in 1795 and staked a claim near Femme Osage Creek in St. Charles County. The north side of the river was more fertile and had more settlements and more attacks from Indians. Many people crossed the river to settle on Tavern, DuBois, St. John's and Boeuf Creeks and Point Labbadie. Lewis and Clark's "Corps of Discovery" camped nearby in 1804.

Washington, Missouri, began when a Revolutionary War veteran, John Long, claimed five thousand arpents at DuBois Creek and a large tract of land at St. John's Creek. A small part of his claim is now within the city of Washington and is the first recorded settlement for the town.

While there are reports of Point Labbadie breaking up as a settlement due to Indian attacks, it appears the majority of the Native Americans were peaceful and friendly. From the discovery of artifacts and arrowheads, it seems that a large number of them lived in the area. The old Maupin Farm, north of Washington, was near a crossing place for the Indians, as was the Achilles Jeffries Farm by Labaddie. Early surveys note the use of Indian trails, listing the "trace that leads east to St. Louis" and the one from "Shawney village on the Burbis River to the Gasconade." Shawneytown was the name of an Indian village in the Bourbeuse Valley.

William G. Owens and his wife, Lucinda Young, are considered the founders of Washington. He was the first postmaster of New Port in 1820 and became the county clerk when New Port was made the county seat. Many people moved from New Port to Union, but the blossoming river trade caught the attention of William Owens.

He acquired several parcels of land, knowing the landing at New Port was poor for river traffic. Union was an inland town, and a natural landing existed at Washington across the Missouri from accessible creeks in Warren County and in between Du Boise and St. John's Creeks. Several ferries ran in the vicinity, and there was a road to Union. Situated at the southernmost bend in the course of the Missouri River, Washington's Landing grew and no one bothered to change its name.

Downtown Washington is said to have developed on fifty acres off the Owenses' property, but trade was carried out at the ferry landing for years and resulted in a small hamlet with a store and other dwellings. German immigrants came to the town and were often referred to as "followers of Gottfried Duden," who lived in Dutzow and wrote "Duden's Letter" describing life in the Missouri Valley. At that time, the streets were dirt footpaths, and there was a mere handful of buildings. The town was invisible from the river until "one was in the midst of it."

Owens was murdered on November 16, 1834, shot in the back as he rode his mule toward the Dobyns Farm. Apparently, John J. Porter, the man who killed Owens, was someone he'd testified against for forging a signature to a real estate transfer. Porter locked himself inside his home, threatening to shoot anyone who approached. He later surrendered when a large number of men accompanied the constable and surrounded his house.

Washington grew after disputes over the property Owens sold before his death. He was a man of substance and promised proper deeds on the payments made for the land he sold. His estate filed suits for clear titles on the land.

The town grew and absorbed the nearby town of Bassora. In 1844, a flood struck and destroyed fields, trees and homes and swept away livestock. Steamboats could not maneuver a landing at the dock against the tide. A cholera epidemic followed, and fevers raged among the survivors of the flood with little relief from medicine.

After construction of the Pacific Railroad, the Forty-Eighters and people moving west for the gold rush increased steamboat traffic until the Hannibal and St. Joseph Railway put an end to river travel. In February 1855, the first train arrived in Washington and was reported on by a young Samuel Clemens (Mark Twain) for the Muscatine, Iowa *Tri-Weekly Journal*.

Ferryboats were no longer needed after 1936, when the bridge spanning the Missouri River connected Washington to Warren County and the towns of Dutzow and Marthasville. Interesting facts about Washington include its zither factory, and the town is known as the "Corn Cob Capital of the World" for the manufacture of corncob pipes.

John B. Busch Brewery

In 1854, John Busch, older brother of Adolphus Busch, built his brewery with Henry Busch and Fred Gersie and by 1860 bottled nearly three thousand kegs of Busch beer aged with beechwood chips and three thousand barrels of ale. Family members worked at the brewery, or provided financial assistance, including Ulrich, Joseph, Henry, George and Adolphus.

John became sole owner in 1894. When the Depression hit, he turned the bottling process into the manufacture of soda pop and potato chips.

John was born John Baptiste Busch in the Rhineland area of Germany in 1832 and came to the United States when he was seventeen. He spent two years training in St. Louis and learned the brewery business from his elder brother George, owner of Busch's Brewery. He attended three years of college at McKendree College in Lebanon, Illinois, and Howard College in Fayette, Missouri. He moved to Washington in 1854.

In 1858, John married Antonie Krumsick. She became vice-president of the company—an unusual position for a woman of the mid-nineteenth century.

Busch's brewery was not the first in the town of Washington. Heinrich Tamm established an early brewery, but John's soon became the largest and remained in operation after Tamm's closed. The building was set into the base of a large hill near the spring-fed Dubois Creek (now Busch Creek). Late in the summer of 1864, Generals Marmaduke, Price, Shelby and Cabell led a wing of the Confederate army from Arkansas into Missouri in what became known as Price's Raid. They encamped at Sullivan on September 30, and the citizens of Washington received warning of their approach.

General Sterling Price and ten thousand of his troops advanced on Washington in September 1864, as he moved toward the state capital of Jefferson City. His men far outnumbered the Union militia of six hundred.

Price himself is not known to have entered the town, but his men looted the town. The residents of Washington and militia under the command of Colonel Dan Gale crossed the Missouri River to the north. The ferryboat took them to safety and then moved on to St. Charles, where it was reported as part of the "Washington Navy." Many refugees hid in the covered bridge at "Quackenbrueck" and were fired upon by the Confederates. None was injured, but bullets lodged in the wooden structure.

Price's men burned the railroad stations and camped outside the brewery, taking whatever they wanted during their one-day raid. It is said that they marched down the streets of the city with their bayonets festooned with stolen hair ribbons. Not satisfied with the looting, they dumped the remainder of the beer before moving on to Jefferson City. The current owners told us on our visit that the men slept inside the large room now used as a restaurant.

Busch filed a claim for damages but never received a penny.

While there have not been any recorded occurrences of a violent nature on the property, there are sightings of a young soldier searching for his missing boot. Orbs are captured on film. Electronic voice phenomenon indicates an intelligent haunting (intelligent hauntings are when the spirits are aware of the presence of the living and attempt to communicate with them). Anomalies show up in photos—strangely shaped lights that appear to have wings. (These could be insects; however, the photos were taken in the area of the brewery where the casks are stored, awaiting shipment. The environment is cold, dark and damp, with rock-lined walls set into the hillside and a cavelike atmosphere.) People have been touched, and growls have been heard.

In the room adjacent to the holding arena, the current owners added a fireplace. During one evening in 2009, a group was investigating the brewery and noticed one of the heavy fireplace pokers swinging with no one standing nearby.

One of the people leading the research was Michael Greeley, who served fourteen years as a certified law enforcement officer in the state of Missouri. He achieved the rank of lieutenant detective and also served as a Drug Abuse Resistance Education (DARE) instructor. He was a member of the sheriff's Emergency Response Team and Drug Enforcement Unit. He received his law enforcement training at the University of Missouri and the Missouri State Highway Patrol.

Greeley is a paranormal investigator from St. Louis. He is a videographer and films documentaries featuring popular paranormal heavyweights like Steven LaChance, Denise Jones and Dr. Michael Henry, among others. Mike has a Warner Bros. credit to his name, professional broadcast videos and recording equipment and many stories about his experiences at the brewery. He's also the creator of WEBX Radio.

His film credits include interviews with Steven LaChance for an episode of the TV show, *Supernatural*. I've met Steven, a survivor of an "extreme haunting," one of a dangerous nature. Steven is widely known for his experience of living in the Union Screaming House and for helping the next tenant deal with the evil presence inside the home. Steven lectures, has been featured in several Booth Brothers documentaries on the paranormal and has written two books, *The Uninvited* and *Crazy*. He's produced his own feature called the *Morse Mill Project* about an old hotel next to Big River. My account on the haunting reported at the Morse Mill Hotel is written in my book *Missouri's Haunted Route 66: Ghosts Along the Mother Road*.

Mike has filmed and witnessed many anomalies at the brewery. One story of Mike's is particularly intriguing. He says he accompanied the investigative group from St. Louis, which had about twenty members present. This group does more than sit in the dark listening for noises. It conducts scientific research using equipment that most paranormal groups can't afford.

That night, Mike was filming with Dan Terry and Dr. Michael Henry inside the Busch Brewery. Dr. Henry conducts ghost tours in St. Charles, Missouri, and wrote the book *Ghosts of St. Charles* for The History Press. I was able to talk with Dr. Henry in St. Louis and learn of his approach to paranormal investigations. His methods focus on the scientific means of explanation.

Mike sent me the following information on the old Washington Brewery:

> *John B. Busch Brewery is rich in history, but little is known about the paranormal activity inside the stone walls of this pre–Civil War establishment. Built in 1854, one mile from the Missouri River in Washington, Missouri, the brewery, also known as JBB (for John Busch Brewery), was established by John and his brother Henry Busch. Together, they formed a partnership with Fred Gersy, who died in 1860. The original name given was Washington Brewery. It wasn't until the mid-1880s that the name was changed to what it's known as today.*
>
> *John B. Busch was seventeen years old in 1849, when he came to America. His father, Ulrick Busch, was a lumber merchant in Hesse-Darmstad, Germany, where John was born in 1832. He is one of twenty-two siblings. His father was married three separate times; the first two wives died. His third wife, Barbara Pfeffer, gave birth to John and his famous younger brother, Adolphus. Adolphus later married into the Anheuser family, thereby forming what is known today as the "King of Beers": the Anheuser Busch dynasty.*

After arriving in the United States, John began work with his older brother George at the Bavarian Brewery in St. Louis, Missouri, where he learned his trade. He didn't know English very well, if at all, so he enrolled in college and studied one year of English at Howard College in Fayette, Missouri.

John married Antonia Krumsick, whose father was a doctor, and together they had seven children, six boys and one girl. Two of their children died as infants. A surviving son was named after his father, Ulrick. His daughter was named Lilly and never married.

John was a member of the Fifty-fourth Missouri Militia, which is also known as the "Home Guard." He received word that the Confederate troops, led by John Sappington Marmaduke, were marching to Washington. He was ordered to board a ferryboat, along with other Home Guard troops, and go upriver to nearby St. Charles, Missouri. The Home Guard was instructed to remain in St. Charles until the Confederate troops had left the area.

While in Washington, General Marmaduke made the brewery their temporary base, and the troops took advantage of the alcohol available to them. Meanwhile, Antonia waited on the general and his men and served them food. Unfortunately, the troops weren't as friendly toward the locals. They set fire to the telegraph station, destroyed the railroad tracks and pilfered. They also killed two people, one a sixteen-year-old boy.

As they continued their march to Jefferson City, the soldiers dumped the remaining beer into a nearby creek, which is now known as Busch Creek. General Marmaduke went to thank Mrs. Busch for her hospitality and dropped a diamond jewel on the floor. She knelt down, picked it up and handed it back to him. He in turn gave it back to her and insisted she keep it. The ring is still in the family. After the Confederate troops left Washington, John returned home with the Home Guard. He sent Washington, D.C., a bill for all the beer he had lost as a result of General Marmaduke's men, but the bill was never paid. At the time of his death in 1894, John was one of the wealthiest people in Washington, Missouri. Two of his sons took over the brewery, one of which was Ulrick. Antonia died in 1906.

During Prohibition of 1918, the equipment from the brewery was sold and shipped to the British Colony of Honduras in South America. To stay in business, Ulrick began producing potato chips, but it almost caused him to lose the family business. Potato chips were an innovative business and were not popular in the 1920s, so sales remained low. He then began to bottle soda and maintained a constant supply of ice, which was mostly sold to Anheuser Busch to keep beer cold on railroad cars. In the late 1920s, he brewed a nonalcoholic beverage he called Buscho.

A third generation of Busches took over the family business during the 1940s. Ulrick I, John's great-grandson, wasn't interested in the brewery business. He wanted to be an architect, so in 1953, after being in business for ninety-nine years, he sent his employees home, and without notice, he shut the doors to the family business for the last time. He went on to fulfill his dream and built schools and many buildings in and around Washington.

John and Antonia's home, mostly built in 1855, sits next to the brewery and was sold to the local Veterans of Foreign Wars (VFW) post. The brewery was sold to a local corncob factory and was used as storage. Rumor has it that it was once filled to the ceilings with corncobs.

Today, the building sits mostly vacant. It has been the site of a variety of businesses. It's locally owned and, more recently, opened to paranormal investigators.

Ghost hunters from all over the country have traveled to conduct investigations, using high-end equipment popular in most investigative techniques. On several occasions, large groups have teamed together to catch a glimpse of a Civil War–era soldier, and there are reports of a small female child, who is often heard laughing and playing. There are reports and photos taken of men standing at the bar. Voices can sometimes be heard during recording sessions. Electromagnetic fields are often detected throughout the building but are more frequent in the large cellar area.

Michael showcases a montage of video footage captured during an investigation conducted in May 2009, featuring a rather heavy and rounded cast-iron fire poker swinging back and forth. The iron poker began swinging by itself and was observed by everyone in attendance. Mike captured several minutes of footage. No breeze was present in the room, and only one of the three fireplace pokers was swinging. Intent in his methods of investigating, he filmed the anomaly from different angles.

He says the group conducted what is known as an EVP session (electronic voice phenomenon), a common procedure in ghost hunting, using a standard recording device such as a digital hand-held recorder. Members of the group randomly asked questions, making an attempt to contact a spirit in the afterlife. EMF (or electromagnetic field) detectors were also used on this occasion; these instruments are believed to detect the presence of energy given by spirits.

A group member asked the spirit if anyone in the audience reminded it of John Busch. Immediately, all the EMF detectors began detecting interference, indicating a positive response. A flashlight, owned by Mr.

Greeley, began flickering on and off. Present was an investigator who had an uncanny resemblance to John Busch.

Setting the flashlight on the floor, the group continued asking questions for approximately ten minutes, with the on-and-off responses indicating they were indeed communicating with an intelligent presence. Mike's account continues:

> *Most frequently, investigators get an opportunity to meet with the spirit of a former employee who reportedly died in the brewery. This employee, who's identified as "Fritz," often makes himself known by either touching or standing close to newcomers in the presence of an orb. Photographs that have orbs often describe them as circular energy or images of light given by spirits.*
>
> *The stone and brick walls, with tunnels leading to the cellar, give a rich elegance of history and charm. The rooms are large, with concave ceilings of brick and mortar. The bar with its dark oak and sculptured horse heads, rich in detail, leaves one to feel relaxed and welcomed. If only these walls could speak—so you may ask, but if you listen, you may hear a voice whispering, willing to tell you all about it.*

John B. Busch Brewery, Washington, Missouri. *Photo by Janice Tremeear.*

The complex consists of three buildings; two served as icehouses. The main building is in five sections, with two large vaulted cellars, a restaurant with banquet facilities and commercial retail and office space. A majority of the complex dates to the late 1800s, and the cellars were part of the original construction.

The middle three-story section faces north. The second-floor windows are twelve-over-twelve sash, and the third-floor windows are six-over-six sash. Inside this section are concrete floors with circular holes that once held the brewing kettles and the industrial staircase. The northwest portion is two stories and once housed the twenty-five-ton ice machine. This section is five bays wide with brick walls and a flat roof.

One feature is a brick corbel table running along the west and northern elevations. A corbel table is a continuous row of corbels (blocks of stone projecting from a wall, supporting some heavy feature of architecture and usually just below the eaves of the roof to give extra support).

The southwest section of the main building is two stories, rectangular and of plain brick. It was the location of the large boilers. Another brick corbel table runs along the length of the south elevation. Here, malt was milled and stored. Grain was spread over paved floors for drying.

In the mid-1880s, John added a steam engine for grinding malt and pumping water. He constructed a lake where he could cut ice during the winter months. John never cared to expand beyond Franklin County and never exceeded production of ten thousand barrels per year.

Beer was produced in the John B. Busch Brewery and Malthouse—or Washington Brewery, as it was also known—until Prohibition in 1918, when it turned to the manufacture of ice, near beer and soda water. The brewery operated for one hundred years, producing products from 1855 to 1954, when it closed.

Fire destroyed most of the complex on July 20, 1888. It is thought that the original cellars remained untouched, and rebuilding brought the brewery back into business within a few months. The main brewery and icehouse were back in place, and a bottling house, an office, a wagon shed, a pump house and a large set of scales occupied the property. An additional icehouse was added in 1898; three more were built later west of the main building, with one on the west side of Dubois Creek. An overhead ice slide extended across Dubois Creek between the two western icehouses. Art Deco sections were put on the main building in 1918 as the beer production halted.

John fought a long illness and died in 1894. His son moved back to Washington and took over the business. The near beer called Buscho became a staple during Prohibition. It was advertised as a "non-intoxicating cereal beverage…a delicious health drink—satisfying liquid food—that can be used daily by all members of the family with good results, all the year around." Unfortunately, Buscho was not popular, and the product was later discontinued.

Like at many of the breweries in St. Louis, Prohibition ruined business, and the Busches sold off the copper kettles and other equipment, filling fifteen or sixteen train cars with goods from the sale. After Prohibition ended, it was too costly to begin the process again, and for the last twenty years the brewery functioned as the bottling and distribution plant for beer produced by the St. Louis Anheuser-Busch Brewery. After the closing of the brew facilities, the Buescher Corncob Pipe Factory rented the building as storage space.

Route 66 Paranormal Alliance was at the John B. Busch brewery in October 2010 with the owners, David and Rhonda Lindauer; Mike Greeley; and members of another research team led by Cheryl (Sherri) Missey.

As we took the tours of the building at dusk, I was followed by a large, shadowy figure. Mike's friend Robin was standing on a platform with Mike and me near a door leading out from the cellars. She suddenly hunched over and felt sick, as though she had been attacked and struck in her midsection.

Our co-founder, Alicia Holder, experienced extreme cold in her right arm during an EVP session with the owner and other people present. Raised veinlike markings appeared along her forearm in full view of all those in the room. Another team member, Andrew Muller, filmed the incident.

Her arm was clammy, frigid and corpselike to the touch as I reached out to trace the vein markings from wrist to elbow. Our EVP session, in conjunction with the pain in Ali's arm, seemed to indicate that a male spirit was attempting contact.

Enoch's Bridge

A discarnate red-haired little girl is one of the ghosts said to haunt this through-truss bridge on Enoch's Knob Road. Straddling Boeuf Creek, the steel structure has two side trusses of iron plates and bars riveted together into triangular and rectangular sections. This metal webbing is connected at the top and bottom and carries the weight of vehicles passing between the trusses. Found between Washington and New Haven, Missouri, this bridge is said to exist within a vortex and carries tales of demon dogs and shadow people in the manner of so many other haunted bridges. Indeed, bridges seem to scare people as much, if not more, than cemeteries. Over the years, these hulking ancients develop lives of their own, born from the whispers brought back into town by teens who party late at night on the dark country roads. Events happen near these steel monsters that often shape a young person's future—or destroy it.

One such tragedy is the case of a young man who went with his buddies to the bridge to take part in the local coming-of-age ritual that youth have always promoted to prove their bravery. The trick here was to climb the webbing of the bridge to the very top.

One version of the story goes like this: a group of young people went to the bridge to perform this act of bravado. The group decided to take a quick trip back into town and left the young man waiting for them. Instead of waiting for his friends to return, he shimmied up the trusses alone.

He slipped, plummeting into the creek thirty to forty feet below.

Another version of the young man's death says that the group left to help someone whose car was stuck. The twenty-three-year-old man, named Patrick, stayed behind. He was recovering from a broken hip, and for reasons unknown, he climbed the trusses. His body was found sometime later that night, and he was pronounced dead from his fall onto the rocks. An accidental death, but his spirit haunts the bridge to this day.

One more version of the story says that Patrick was attending a party at the bridge, and witnesses saw him climb the trusses, but no one saw him fall. His body was seen lying broken on the jagged rocks below. Some say Patrick assumes the form of a dog when he makes his appearance on the bridge. Red eyes glow from the surrounding woods since Patrick Kinnison's death. However, animals' eyes will glow when illuminated by light. Are the glowing eyes paranormal or a trick of an active imagination?

Patrick may have been taking pain medication after the surgery on his hip. He loved climbing, even as a child. Reports say the hip injury was from a fall while climbing. The night he fell off Enoch's Bridge, he was medicated and under the influence of alcohol.

Often, empty beer containers are found in the vicinity. This influence may be a leading cause of the many reports of paranormal activity on the bridge.

Built about 1908 at a length of 185 feet and a width of 15 feet, the bridge is now declared structurally deficient. Its weight limit is three tons. There are tracks running along the length of the wooden deck. It runs parallel to State Highway 100, and the railroad gives the illusion of being in the middle of nowhere. Other stories tell about young men hanging themselves from the bridge or jumping to their doom over lost love.

Enoch's Bridge, near Washington, Missouri. Note the unknown mist forming at the right side of photo. *Photo by Janice Tremeear.*

A full moon on Friday the Thirteenth brings out strange creatures to climb the trees and specters of dogs chasing those on or near the bridge, disappearing as suddenly as they appear. Signs on the bridge are torn down (pranksters or ghosts?).

Mists are seen and photographed, along with dark masses and apparitions. Cars stalled on the bridge when it was open to traffic (it is now blocked and slated for destruction). A rumor of a phantom building accompanies the haunting around the bridge. The building burned to the ground but can often be seen restored.

A small child is also said to have fallen through the bridge; this is unproven, but there is a large metal plate bolted to the deck. Screams of women and children are reported in the woods. Wild animals, as well as domestic ones, roam the area. Coyotes and owls can make cries that may sound like a child's cry or a human scream.

Another death at the bridge was that of forty-one-year-old Stephen Cooksey, who was killed on May 9, 2005, in a drug transaction that went wrong. He was shot multiple times with a .22 yet dragged himself beneath his car for safety. His car was set on fire with Cooksey beneath.

I was at Enoch's Bridge in October 2010 with the Route 66 Paranormal Alliance, Mike Greeley, Robin Williams and Cheryl Missey. We stood on the bridge and experienced a sense of vertigo, also reported by others when in the middle of the bridge. Paranormal, or a fun house effect brought on by the darkness, the water below and the wind blowing between the trusses?

Mike Greeley, alliance member Ali and I walked into the woods alongside Beouf Creek, following a beaten-down path. Mike paused at a certain spot and asked us if we "got" anything there. I was facing back the way we came, taking photos of the area.

Drawn to my right, I stared at a place by a tree with brambles twisting behind it, blocking the creek from view. I felt as if the place was significant; a shudder passed over me. I knew something had occurred here. "This is where it happened," Mike said. "Right there," he pointed to where I felt the pull, "is the spot the burned car was found."

Mike gave me the following account of one night he was filming at the bridge:

If there is one location in the Missouri Ozarks that is synonyms with paranormal activity, it's Enoch's Knob Bridge. Built around 1908, this truss bridge is one of the most visited bridges in the Midwest by ghost hunters. It's located on Enoch's Knob Road, which is about six miles west of Washington, Missouri. It's a favorite hangout among the local teenagers and would-be ghost hunters. There are stories about a three-legged dog suddenly appearing after a ritual is performed, which includes parking one's vehicle in the middle of the bridge, shutting off the motor and lights. One is to honk their horn three times, flash their headlights three times and start the motor. Once you turn the headlights on a final time, a three-legged dog is to appear. I have witnessed this ritual done over a dozen times in three years and have failed to observe a three-legged dog—although the suspense is exciting to watch. Everyone seems to get a laugh out of the ritual; however, I spoke to a local, who says a three-legged dog did appear for him, but he felt it was coincidental, and it didn't look like a ghost.

I recall the first time I was at the bridge and my baseball cap was lifted off my head. Seconds later, a full-body apparition, witnessed by many, was observed running from where I was standing toward the opposite end of the bridge, when it dissipated into thin air. Unfortunately, I didn't have my camera recording for this experience. The fact that several people saw it validates my story.

Over the years, I've witnessed people getting shoved, slapped, hearing voices, foul odors (which smelled like a decaying body), shadow figures, vehicle dome lights turning on, to name a few, but there is one incident I will never forget.

On August 7, 2010, after finishing up a previous investigation a little early in nearby Washington, I decided to accompany a group of investigators to the bridge. About thirty minutes into the investigation, an investigator, who was making her first visit, and I began to lose our balance. It was like I had just gotten off a merry-go-round. I remained alert but had little control over my body. The female investigator experienced the same effect; however, the remaining two investigators did not experience the disorienting feeling.

The experience was felt only after we stepped off the bridge and onto the gravel roadway. The two of us returned to the bridge, and the disorienting feeling subsided almost immediately. We walked from one end of the bridge to the other; however, when we decided to leave, the feeling came back, but this time it was stronger!

One of the investigators who wasn't experiencing the effects decided to conduct an EVP session. She used a digital recorder, and while holding an EMF detector, she stood next to the female investigator and me. Immediately, she began to experience interference with the EMF detector as it began to flicker off and on. She began to question its reasoning, and it was then that I began hearing a hum, and then a loud burst of energy exploded at our feet! It was powerful enough to shake the entire bridge. It was like a bomb or cannon.

I have a recording of the incident, and it's totally an anomaly of massive proportions! On the recording, you can hear the bridge reverberate as everyone was taken aback by the experience. It was like time stopped! Everyone was taken aback by the experience. I wanted to leave. It's my belief, when one experiences such a traumatic event, there may be something much worse coming.

My hunch was correct. My experience didn't end at the bridge. The other investigator and I suffered weeks of severe depression, fatigue and illness. In addition, I experienced much worse, but refused to talk in depth about it. It's disturbing and I don't want to experience it again! What I experienced, I took home to my family, and it didn't only affect me but it affected them too.

Although there are two confirmed deaths reported as happening at the bridge, one an accidental death and another a homicide, it is believed by many who investigate the site that there are more unrecorded deaths. Acting on a tip given to me, I did some research and found an article in the Franklin County Record, *dating Thursday, July 17, 1879, which indicated a gentleman by the name of William Peters and his twelve-year-old son drowned at the site. Their bodies were discovered after a neighbor observed a wagon abandoned. A search was conducted, and the bodies were found in the rain-swollen creek. The paper states their bodies were immediately buried where they were found. The* Franklin County Record *also reports the "creek has again offered a sensation and a horror by engulfing two more unwary victims in its murky depths."*

This statement leads me to believe there were more deaths reported at this site.

On August 17, 2010, Enoch's Knob Bridge was deemed unsafe and was subsequently shut down. The Franklin County Commission decided to tear it down and relocate a new bridge in a different location. Enoch's Knob was once known as Steiner's Ford Bridge.

Mike says he has filmed at Enoch's Knob Bridge over a dozen times in the past three years. He says it's one of his favorite sites because he and the groups he escorts usually experience some sort of anomaly.

PHELPS COUNTY

Now it is that time of night,
That the graves all gaping wide,
Every one lets forth his sprite,
In the church-way paths to glide.
—*Puck in Shakespeare's* A Midsummer Night's Dream

ROLLA

Rolla sits snugly in the south central highland of the Ozarks along old Route 66, strategically located between St. Louis, Jefferson City, Columbia and Springfield. The premier technological research facility, Missouri University of Science and Technology (formerly the Missouri School of Mines and the University of Missouri–Rolla) is a college many strive to enter. A mini Stonehenge constructed by university students sits on campus. A little-known fact of the campus is that it harbors a nuclear reactor. The school created and perfected the technique of water cutting stone. Sophomores in medical engineering conduct courses in robot technology, and many graduates have been hired by companies such as Boeing, even during hiring freezes. Lieutenant James Albert led the survey that mapped out the railroad at Rolla, and he became the first professor of civil engineering at the Missouri School of Mines.

The first settlers came in the early 1800s; they were farmers and ironworkers following the Meramec, Gasconade and Little Piney Rivers.

John Webber built his home in what was to become Rolla in 1844. Edward Bishop settled here nine years later and is considered the founder of Rolla, which achieved town recognition in 1858.

A folk legend of how Rolla gained its name comes from the battle for the county seat with Dillion. Rolla won, and the citizens of Dillion were given the opportunity to choose the name for the new county seat. In a spirit of ill will, they chose to name the city Rolla after a worthless hunting dog.

The non-fabled account says that the first choice came from Webber, who wanted the name Hardscrabble for the clay dirt in the area. Bishop meanwhile wanted the name Phelps Center, as the city is in Phelps County. However, new settlers, who arrived from North Carolina and missed their hometown Raleigh, chose the city name with a different spelling: Rolla.

The Frisco Line connected Rolla and St. Louis in 1861. Even with the war putting a temporary end to westward expansion, the town was a hub of activity and transportation for supplies from the east. According to the *Rolla Express* on December 3, 1869:

> *Rolla will be the center for the southwestern trade of this State and Northern Arkansas. All the big ox-wagons and fine mule teams that swarm past our office windows every day, on their way to Dillion for freight will before many days back up to this place to load. Every one of these people and wagons, all these oxen, mules and horses are to be accommodated. Besides, newcomers are every day drifting this way, some prospecting, others to sojourn with us for a season, and some to make it their permanent abode.*

A military post was established during the Civil War with about twenty thousand Union troops stationed in the vicinity. Rolla was a major city along old Route 66 when the road replaced the near impassable graveled Route 14. Route 66 became a concrete slab in 1928 between Rolla and Lebanon. It took a fair amount of time to complete. Soon, Rolla became a vacation playground with tourist cabins, trading posts (such as the still-standing Mule Trading Post) and fishing camps. Access to the Current River and Jack's Fork Rivers attract outdoorsmen to the town.

Diane Marie Henke is the curator of the Phelps County Museum. She works in what was originally the Missouri Trachoma "Eye" Hospital, followed by the Highway Patrol Academy and others. It has been Rock Mechanics & Explosives Research Center since the mid-1970s. EVPs have been captured, orbs have been seen through camera lenses and there have been reports of touching—all the usual haunted activities. The former

Entering Rolla, Missouri, on Route 66. Vintage postcard. *Courtesy Janice Tremeear.*

hospital was constructed in 1939 to fight trachoma, which spread from Kentucky to eastern Oklahoma. The disease affects the eye and is the leading cause of blindness in the United States. On July 1, 1957, the highway patrol gained control of the facility and turned it into a training school for the state law enforcement agency. For a year and a half, a small section of the location served as an outpatient clinic for trachoma patients and children with cerebral palsy.

The building became part of the Missouri University of Science and Technology's Rock Mechanics & Explosives Research Center after closing as a hospital. What ghosts exist there are unknown, but the former hospital is not the only historical site in Rolla with legendary haunts.

The courthouse was the second public structure completed after Rolla became county seat; the first was the jail, which also boasts tales of ghosts within its walls, according to Diane. Rolla was known as a rough-and-tumble railroad town, which may explain the activities of the older buildings. After all, malefactors required the security of a good, stout stone building to keep them off the streets and away from the innocent public.

Resting on bricks of dolomite quarried locally, the courthouse walls were of bricks molded in the Rolla area. The structure's exterior was complete, but the interior remained unfinished as the Civil War hit Missouri. Union troops seized Rolla in June 1861 and stored hay and oats in the building. Military officers later took over to establish offices and a military hospital on the site. Thirteen cells, six by thirteen feet, on the lower floor for solitary confinement held both military and civilian prisoners during the Civil War. The upper floor held a single room with cages fit with iron bars to hold multiple prisoners. A wood stove on the upper floor actually aided an escape at one point because of the building's thatched roof.

One prisoner is reported having been put to death at the courthouse.

Diane Henke's son Jason told me the story of Rolla's most infamous villain. George Bohernman killed a man in nearby Newburg in a scuffle over a woman. George was held in the Phelps Courthouse and executed by hanging just a block or two from the courthouse at the Rolla Cemetery.

Vault wings were added in 1881 on both sides of the courthouse, and by 1912 the old 1860 jail was emptied and transferred to the new wing of the courthouse.

During the Depression, the courthouse became dilapidated as the flow of money waned. The belfry was dismantled in 1950, and the Phelps County Postwar Development Committee decided that a new building was in order. Voters resisted, and improvements of a drop ceiling, a new brick addition and a mezzanine floor were included in the building's design. Several attempts to raze the 130-year-old courthouse failed, and eventually the building was placed on the National Register of Historic Places in 1990.

Missouri is crisscrossed with many roads bearing legends of supernatural activity, including Hillsboro Road in Festus, with its haunted railroad crossing; Dark Hollow Road, aka Devil's Hollow Road, a seven-mile stretch of gravel situated between Fulton and the town of Ham's Prairie. The road is known for the panther (or "creature") of Dark Hollow Road, ghost headlights that pass through cars, cold spots, odd sounds, screams, odd moving shapes, glowing graves and the young couple who died in a drunken car crash on the road. There's also the tale of the motorcyclist who disappeared, except for his bike and one boot with his leg still inside.

Satan's Tunnel just north of Warrenton is well known by residents in the area. Rumors of this location include the ghost of a man killed on the tracks, devil worshippers and the whistle of a train on the bridge over the road where no train runs any longer. A witch is said to live in the woods near a graveyard, and an old one-room school nearby is haunted.

As teenagers, my daughter Charlene Wells, now a member of Route 66 Paranormal Alliance, and her friend Martha Robbins took a trip after dark to the tunnel and came back scared and shaken by sounds and lights they witnessed inside. But when Charlene and Martha came back, the girls weren't alone. Standing outside in my front yard was a large, shadowy man. He hovered beneath the streetlamp, fully illuminated, waiting for Martha to leave my house and head for home. They believed he had followed them from their excursion at Satan's Tunnel.

Taylor Road by Blue Springs has the tale of a ghost girl on the road who haunts the location where she was thrown from a car and died.

Nine-Mile Bridge at Kingdom City has ghosts of slaves hung from the bridge. They are seen on the bridge, and if you sit and dangle your feet over the sides, you'll feel a tickling on the bottom of your feet. This locale has all the earmarks of other reported ghost sightings—lights, shadows, screams— but Nine-Mile also has the sobbing of someone truly sad and alone.

Zombie Road, once old Lawler Road and now the Al Foster walking trail, is in Wildwood in South County, St. Louis, formerly the town of Glenco. This past October, I was there with my team, the Route 66 Paranormal Alliance, and Tom Halstead, the man whose photo of shadow children standing along a ridge was featured in the Booth Brothers documentary *Children of the Grave*. Zombie Road is one of the most widely known haunted locations in the state of Missouri. Tom's photo caught the attention of Philip and Christopher Booth and has captured the interest of everyone who has seen the shadow children Tom photographed. The odd thing about Tom's photo is that the children are clearly seen lining the ridge, but there are no reflections of the shadowy figures in the water directly below. Zombie Road has a long, multi-hued history that included being a route for Civil War soldiers. When we walked the road that night, we came to a wide, flat area, and I received an impression of a tent city spread out over the ground. At that time, I didn't know about the soldiers who used the old pathway during the war. More can be read on Zombie Road in *Missouri's Haunted Route 66: Ghost Along the Mother Road*.

One of Missouri's haunted roads is Spook Hollow Road.

Spook Hollow Road

Brandi Ousley, familiar with Rolla, tells the following story of a well-known haunt:

> It dead ends down to an abandoned cemetery (if I think right, I do believe it's Pine Hill). One of the stories is that there was a group of people going into the cemetery to do rituals and perform sacrifices. Some of the children used in the sacrifices can be heard the closer you get to the cemetery, and you can see distant light blue flames as you drive up to the cemetery. The little

log cabin on the bluff is said to house the adults who were involved with these sacrifices. And let me tell ya, it's a creepy little place.

At the end of Spook Hollow Road is the place the locals know as Goatman's Grave. Dean Pestana, a member of the Route 66 Paranormal Alliance and a former resident of Rolla, told his story of the infamous goatman in Missouri's *Haunted Route 66: Ghosts Along the Mother Road.* This individual is described as a satyr, with the top half being a man and the bottom half a goat.

Interestingly enough, goatmen are reported in many states throughout North America. Legend states that the very first goatman was seen in Maryland, in the forested areas. He is seen along a bridge and two other roads and can be heard giving a shrill cry that sounds like the cry of a baby. Animals are reported missing at the hands of the goatman with mutilated carcasses discovered after sightings.

A seven-foot-tall version haunts the roads of Alabama. Eastern Texas had a report in 1972, and California has its "Chevo (Spanish word for goat) Man." Oregon, Oklahoma and Kentucky, and even New Zealand, lay claim to the goatman. Much like the urban legend of the "man with a hook" the goatman stalks teenagers from across the world in parked cars along lonely highways. The suburbs of Washington, D.C., reported a twelve-foot-tall goatman prowling the region.

Brandi continues her tale of Spook Hollow Road and the Goatman's Grave at its end:

Goatman's Grave has always been a favorite for us to go to. It's out at Pine Hill Cemetery (Pine Hill Road), out in St. James, on this really rough, old, gravel road. Now, there are people who say goatman is a myth, an urban legend of some type; then there are those who have actually seen and caught on film an apparition of what looks like a man, with hooves for feet. Personally, I've never come across him, but I have had some very not-so-settling happenings at the cemetery. Cemetery grounds are hallow grounds, as we all know, and are usually rough terrain to walk on; not this one—you sink. I've had my shirt caught on fire. I've been pushed. I've blacked out and couldn't remember anything until we were closer to town. We have been stuck out by the cemetery entrance with a dead car because it would not turn over, but at sunrise it started and drove out just fine. One of the girls who was with me, she has a scar on her right hand from something making its mark. We have recordings of something saying, like it was sitting right next to me, "Get out," and have heard what sounded like a horse running after us as were bookin' butt back to the truck. Talk about entertaining! The last time we went out there, we weren't there long; it was daylight, and we were taking some pics and doing some recordings when Lynn noticed a small altar set up on the back old rock gravesides. The butcher knife had blood on it that had dried. I made a quick decision that we should leave, and quickly. Lol!

The abandoned bus on Highway T is another one people say is a myth, but when you got someone/something chasing you from the shadows screaming, "I'll Kill you!" you tend not to think it's fake. There was a homeless guy who used to live in it; he was not run out—he was allowed to stay—and died in the bus. It got too cold and he couldn't get warm. People say the red eyes you see through the bus windows are old beer bottles. I've been up inside that bus; there aren't any beer bottles, and there is the makeshift bed the homeless guy stayed in and a whole bunch of old newspapers and old tuna cans and stuff like that. The shadow that chased us was indeed that, a shadow; it wasn't a person, or anything like that. Chased us up the hill for a good half a mile. We turned around and went back to check and see if it was possibly the neighbor, but no one was there; no vehicles, no anything that looked like it would of disturbed the neighbors was anywhere to be seen. I still have that original tape from that—that and the photos on one of my flash drives.

There is no access allowed to the cemetery at night. There is a map to the Pine Hill Cemetery that most people now associate with the Goatman's Grave, but is that his preferred place of terrorism or does he move about the county?

Dean told me of his knowledge of the goatman sightings that took place west of Rolla. Pine Hill Cemetery lies east of Rolla and south of St. James. On September 19, 2010, we drove to Rolla to interview people for stories to be included in this book. We drove out Highway E to Randy's Roadkill BBQ, past split rail fences and the bones of stripped cedars trees that had outlived their former glory as someone's Christmas trees and now dotted the ditches next to the woods. Randy's sits near the road at the end of a plein-air setting, perfect for the budding artist to set up easel and canvas. A pond is behind the restaurant in a rolling pasture, and Randy's home sits tucked even farther back, sheltered by trees. Randy was chatting with customers on the open deck as they enjoyed their lunch. Periodically, he shooed away the Canadian geese that begged for leftovers. Dean and I introduced ourselves to Randy when he entered his restaurant and told him I was collecting local ghost stories for this book. He said one of his employees could help us and went into the kitchen to send Jason Henke our way.

While we waited, I bought a Roadkill T-shirt in a blindingly green color and asked for a printed menu as a bit of a souvenir. A few of the choice items were Dead Chicken Chunks (boneless); opossum tail with one side (a deep-fried, bacon-wrapped hotdog) and armadillo tail with a side (deep-fried, bacon-wrapped Cajun sausage).

Jason has heard similar tales about the goatman—that he is seen on the western side of town—and as far as Jason knew, the "Goatman's Grave" location was unknown. Here is a perfect example of how urban legends grow with time, and with each telling they change to take on a life of their own.

Jason had this to say: "One night a man was driving down Highway E and crashed into a tree. Later he told officers he wrecked his car because the goatman jumped out at him from the woods."

This was supposed to have happened a few miles from where we sat with our Roadkill lunch.

Jason also said there was an old tale of an African American church, location unknown, that had been burned to the ground by white supremacists with the congregation still inside. Their ghosts are said to haunt the site.

Another historic site in Rolla is on the corner of Third and Rolla Streets. The John A. Dillion Log House was once the first Phelps County Courthouse. Built in 1857, it was both a Union hospital in the Civil War and a storage supply warehouse. The log home is a two-story museum haunted by Maude, a lady who worked there until her death. Maude dressed in period clothing for tourists and is seen wearing her costume. Objects are moved in the home, batteries are drained and electronic equipment fails. Soldiers are reported in the museum, but all seem benign in temperament.

Brandi Ousley offers another personal ghost story from Rolla:

At the train track on Rolla Street and Third, there was a little girl back in the 1800s who got mad at her mother's decisions and decided to run away from home. There was a train that was coming down the tracks, and she got her foot stuck and couldn't move in time. Till this day, around the fall time and a little closer to the holidays, you can see at a certain time at night an old lantern swaying back and forth down the tracks. The closer you get, the dimmer the light gets, and once you're on top of it, it's gone.

Parallel Cemetery is a pet name all of us have given it who grew up around these stories. You go out Y Highway (where Briggs and Stratton used to be) and keep going till you get to Kokomo Joe's; there is a cemetery on the right and a road to the left. You take the road to the left, till you come up on what is now a chain-linked little cemetery. People disappear at that cemetery, and this last disappearance caused the cemetery caretakers to fence it in.

The first happened to a guy we all (class of 2002) went to school with, one of our best buds. He lived right up the road from this cemetery, and we all went out there to have a small get-together (we were not partying believe it or not). We kept hearing footsteps and rustling in the woods and weird sounds. Some got pushed, I got tripped and some other people were shoved around. Patrick (the one who disappeared) did just that—we were talking to him one second and the next second he was gone. Two weeks later, he comes to school in the same clothes we last seen him in. He looked like the walking dead! Had cuts and scrapes and was covered in dirt. We asked him what happened, and he hadn't a clue. He said he woke up and was sitting outside the school.

The second caused the cemetery to be fenced in. There were some kids out there drinking and partying, and they had shovels and were tearing up the place. A neighbor, catty-corner from the cemetery, said she heard screaming and someone yelling, "Help!" and "No, stop it! We didn't mean it!" When the cops got there, they found the two shovels and the flashlights…and body drag marks all over the area, but the two boys weren't anywhere around. Still, to this day, mind you it happened earlier this summer, they have never been found. These two stories sound crazy, but it really happened. We have all been out there, taken pictures, gotten voice recording of something in a hushed mumble, "Come here pretties, we wanna play" or "Don't go into the dark, they never come out of the dark." I haven't been our there in months. (Can have fifteen-plus people verify these stories.)

Houston House, Newburg

Newburg (population five hundred) is home to a former railroad roundhouse adjacent to the Little Piney River and a part of old Route 66 history.

The "Mother Road" was commissioned on November 11, 1926, and snakes through eight states, from Chicago, Illinois, to Santa Monica, California. It is twenty-four hundred miles long; three hundred miles of the road in Missouri are called "Bloody 66" due to the numerous accidents that occurred on the dark, curved and hilly road. Route 66 spans ten counties in Missouri and followed an ancient dirt path on a ridge trod by migrating mastodon. It roughly followed the old Osage Indian Trail taken as the Indians searched for game.

The white man knew the trail as the St. Louis–Springfield Road, and the old path played a strategic part in the Civil War for the transportation of men and materials. When telegraph wires were strung along its course, it became the "Wire Road" until the designation Route 66 was assigned.

Small now, Newburg was a boomtown built to house railroad workers and their families. Developed by the Frisco Railroad, it was baptized with a birthday of 1884 by its citizens. William Painter is the man who surveyed near Little Piney Creek to establish the town, naming it Newburgh. In 1888, the post office changed the stock place name when the town became incorporated (the name means, of course, new town or village).

Rolla was the first choice for the Frisco Line, but the city refused to donate land to the railroad, knowing the history of the less-than-permanent cities that sprang up with such endeavors. Businesses soon followed the railroad, and the building of the oldest structure in town, the Railroad Eating-House, joined the tents that made up the town. Opened in 1884, the hotel/restaurant offered workers a place to eat and sleep.

Serving as a division point, Newburg's roundhouse supplied "helper" engines to aid the heavy steam locomotives climb the steep grades to the east and west. Railroad jobs attracted many people to the area, and the town prospered within a few short months. Five grocery stores and many hotels lined the streets. The population became three times the size of the current town. Traffic officers were needed to patrol the streets and control the flow of movement.

A theater was constructed in the era of silent movies on the same block as the Railroad Eating-House, now named the Houston House. Next door to the Lyric Theater is the Sullivan Hotel, constructed soon after the Houston House.

William James organized the Ozark Iron Works, which built a large furnace west of Newburg to help offset the antiquated technology of the Maramec Iron Works. Rail transportation allowed iron deposits from Phelps County to travel to other markets and led to a boom in mining and the production of fire clays. Timber and farm products profited by the rail system.

The Houston House is now undergoing a renovation project to preserve it and to help restore the community that has faded with the passing of the railroad and I-44's replacement of Route 66. Ghost hunts are offered at the restaurant, where EVPs have been captured and tales are told of a train delivering people who never left the old hotel. The familiar haunts are here: disembodied voices, cold spots and signs of someone or something attempting to communicate with those still living. The old building was

Houston House, Newburg, Missouri. *Photo by Mark Dean.*

established during a rough-and-tumble time in Missouri's history. It doesn't take much to imagine the hardy rail workers gathering at the hotel to rest, play cards and perhaps stir up some trouble.

At this time, the Newburg Community Revitalization Program Group (NCRPG) owns the Houston House and operates a senior citizens' center and soup kitchen, offers classes and computer banking, runs a caring center and houses the Children's Museum in the annex to the restaurant. The NCRPG is negotiating the purchase of the former roundhouse property to redevelop the twenty-eight acres into a park, recreation area and rail museum, bringing tourism back to Newburg. It's hoped that the shuttered storefronts, weed-infested lots and silent streets will once again make way for the bustling of human traffic.

PULASKI COUNTY

To put money into the foundation of a building brings luck.

If a person experiences great horror, his hair turns white.

A person born on Halloween will have the gift of communicating with the dead.

If the flame of a candle flickers and then turns blue, there's a spirit in the room.

Sparrows are thought to carry the souls of the dead,
and it is believed to bring bad luck if you kill one.

In the days before the gallows, criminals were hanged from the top rung of a
ladder, and their spirits were believed to linger underneath. Common folklore
says it's bad luck to walk beneath an open ladder and pass through
the triangle of evil ghosts and spirits.

—Various superstitions

Pulaski County was founded in 1833 and named for the Polish Patriot Count Casimir Pulaski. The original county contained what are now the counties of Laclede, Wright, most of Dallas, Webster, Phelps, Texas Camden and Miller. The area drew tourists and sportsmen for over a century, as well as the U.S. Army, which built the Fort Leonard Wood training center.

CRY BABY HOLLOW

Dave Harkins, founder/co-director of the Ozarks Paranormal Society, based near Lebanon/Lake of the Ozarks, sent me the following information on a location north of Waynesville, Missouri:

Known to have a quantity of haunted locations, Cry Baby Hollow near Crocker is one of the most told stories and one the locals know in one form or another. Many versions of the haunting exist, but few have the true facts due to the age of the tales. One of the oldest known stories is that a house once stood in the area of Cry Baby Hollow. Large cedar trees, common around old homesteads, surrounded the house. A toddler wandered away from the house and became lost.

A storm blew up, and search was difficult for the child. The mother, refusing to give up, continued searching for her child and, like the toddler, succumbed to the elements. At night, you can hear the child crying and see the apparition of the mother searching the woods for her child. Other, lesser-known tales include: If you are in Cry Baby Hollow between 11:50 p.m. and 12:20 a.m., you'll see a flash of light as if a door is opening. A baby's cries and screams are heard, as well as the mother crying out for her child. Red eyes appear in various spots in the woods around you. Rumors are that the woman was also pregnant, and while searching for the toddler, she fell into a ravine and was dead when rescuers found her.

Version three is that a woman riding in a wagon with her baby was coming home from a party. The horses were spooked and bolted, throwing them both from the wagon. The horses trampled the mother and child, and on certain nights you can hear them both screaming and crying in the woods.

The woods are said to be the gateway to hell, and many people who brave the night in the hollow have vehicle trouble as they exit the woods, experiencing flat tires, mysterious claw marks and a child's handprints on the vehicle—even wrecks!

Jason Henke agrees with the legends of Cry Baby Hollow and its legends of crying children.

Several locations across the United States have cry baby legends—hills, graveyards, roads, bridges, hollows—all places that are remote and removed from public areas. Each has a similar tale: babies or children lost, killed or abandoned and haunting the location. Many times, car trouble is experienced on or near the spot of the haunting. Handprints appear on the vehicles, and sometimes claw marks, and screams and cries of children and their mothers can be heard.

Cry Baby Hollow carries the mystique of being cursed by either a witch or a vengeful gypsy seeking her revenge on the townspeople who accused her children of stealing chickens.

A half-human, half-cat child is seen there. The surrounding land is cursed as well. Odd fogs and colored mists are reported.

There are old stories is of a woman whose car stalled at the hollow. She left the car to get help and, upon returning, found her child missing and blood everywhere. Ever since, cars entering the area die.

Older people of the community recognize the location as being haunted but are afraid to speak of it. Bad luck seems to befall those who live nearby, with cattle dying and children becoming sick. Crop failure is blamed on the cursed land.

The pregnant woman story continues with her returning home from town and losing a buggy wheel while crossing the creek. She couldn't carry her oldest child and left the youngster sleeping in the buggy while she went to fetch help. Upon her return, the child was missing, and blood covered the buggy. Beside herself with grief, she ran into the woods, searching and screaming for her child. Her body was discovered the next day.

The tale varies slightly from a mother throwing her child over the bridge to a mother and child being tossed out of a wagon (Cry Baby Hollow, Crocker). Some legends claim that Indians killed their deformed young at these waterways; others say mulatto children met a similar fate to hide the interaction between slaves and their white owners (Nine-Mile Bridge).

There are tales of school buses crashing, killing the children (Monmouth, Illinois), and cars skidding off icy roads and parents losing a child in the frozen water (Dublin, Indiana).

Naturally, with time the legend grows. Each new thrill-seeker who hears a coyote yelping in the woods or leaves rustling nearby with the passing of an animal in the dark jumps with the tales firmly etched into his or her mind and brings back new tales of horror encountered out in the woods.

Experiencing a ghost can be a harrowing occurrence for many, but imagine the sorrow that touches all of us over the death of a child. Discarnate babies and children are by far creepier than ghosts of adults. We want those little spirits to move on into the light, to not be bound to earth or continued suffering. And thanks to Hollywood, ghosts of children are extremely scary. How frantic is it to hear the unearthly screams of a mother searching for her lost child until she, too, succumbs to the elements and dies alone and frightened. How unnerving to hear the cries and wails of children and babies weeping in fear and begging to be found. Or those children rumored to have been killed by their parents—what sounds of pleading and terror did they make?

In doing research for this book, I came across an unusually gruesome and inventive way of committing suicide. No wonder Missouri has such a high number of ghosts running about. According to the *Old Stagecoach Stop Gazette*, reprinted from the *Pulaski County Democrat*, August 1, 1902:

> *Just after 7 o'clock last night persons about the Laclede Hotel and on the street were horrified to see a man jump into the smokestack of an eastbound freight engine standing at the new watering place at the east end of the depot. The man climbed up on the rear-end of the engine and up on top of the headlight and deliberately jumped feet first into the smokestack. For a few moments the upper part of his body remained in view over the top of the smokestack and then sank out of view. As soon as possible the trainmen unbolted the smokestack and it was tipped back over on the boiler. The body had settled down so that about half of it was in the smokestack and half in the lower part below. A rope was passed around the body and it was pulled out but life was extinct and the flesh burned.*
>
> *From letters found in his clothing the suicide is supposed to be Owen Greelish and has a brother living in Chicago and another in Leavenworth, Kan. Messages were sent to them, but up to the time of going to press no word has been received from them.*

The method of suicide adopted to end his life was a most sensational one—and probably the first time such a means has been resorted to.

BENTON, CAMDEN, MILLER AND MORGAN COUNTIES

A granny woman in the Ozarks could tell of birthing babies born with two faces, with one ear, with hooflike feet, pop eyes and many other abnormal conditions. In her wisdom, she will always have a plausible explanation for the abnormalities.
—Ozark folklore

Undoubtedly, one of the most fascinating aspects of Ozarks oral tradition are tales of the fabled "blood stoppers," a group of healers who claimed the power to halt the unnatural flow of blood.
—Folklore tradition

LAKE OF THE OZARKS

Many towns in mid-Missouri now reside at the bottom of the dragon-shaped Lake of the Ozarks. Over fifty-four thousand acres are swallowed by the meandering waterway fed by three ancient rivers: the Osage, the Big and Little Nianguas and the Glaize. Cliffs of Ozarks bedrock border it on all sides. Caves and springs are hidden among the forests and hills.

"Paradise" is the word most often used; it was first utilized by the Persians to describe luxurious summer resorts around the Persian Gulf. Later, the Greeks borrowed the word for the same purpose.

In the 1930s and '40s, people came to the forested shores of the lake to forget their troubles—the Depression and World War II. The '50s and '60s became a

Moonlight scene at Lake of the Ozarks, Missouri. Vintage postcard. *Courtesy Janice Tremeear.*

more romantic time at the lake as many mom-and-pop ventures cropped up like anthills, attracting families discovering the beauty of life on the water.

Wild animal parks sprang up, show caves opened and gravity-defying mystery houses drew in crowds. Ski shows packed in parents and kids. I've watched the acrobatic skiers balancing on shoulders while building a moving pyramid. Growing up with a love of musicals, being at the water show was as close to watching Esther Williams in the flesh as I was likely to get.

What ghosts haunt the flooded towns? Do ghosts in fact haunt a town that is now under water?

One of the more widely known and popular haunted locations is Bridal Cave.

Within the Osage tribe, many smaller tribes existed. Conwee was the son of Chief Neongo of the Big Hills, a tribe of the Osage who lived on the north shore of what is now Ha Ha Tonka State Park. He fell in love with Wasena, daughter of Elkhorn, chief of the Little Hills. This tribe lived on the north side of the Osage, near the junction of the Niangua. Conwee desired Wasena as his wife, but Wasena and her father did not favor the young man.

Conwee was not discouraged, and one night he took men with him to cross the Osage. He kidnapped Wasena and her friend Irona.

At dawn, they hid in a cave to avoid being seen by their pursuers, and Wasena was able to escape her captors. She ran toward the edge of a cliff two hundred feet above the Niangua River. As Conwee nearly had her within his grasp, she sprang from the cliff without so much as a backward glance, choosing death over marriage to a man she did not love. The cliff has been called Lover's Leap ever since.

Irona had been in love with Prince Buffalo, Conwee's brother, for some time, and after mourning the death of Wasena, Irona married Prince Buffalo inside the cave where the two women had been held captive. The ceremony took place in a beautiful room called the Bridal Chapel, and the cave was given the name Bridal Cave. The haunting tales associated with the Bridal Cave and Thunder Mountain Park include chanting and singing by the Osage Indians, along with drumbeats and the occasional appearance of Native American apparitions.

If you search, you can find other urban tales of ghosts lurking along the lake's edge. Laurie, Missouri, is tucked in the dragon's spine of the lake. It's a vacation paradise, but

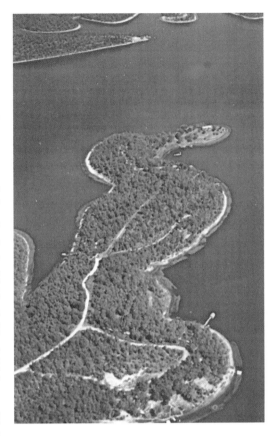

Duckhead Point at Lake of the Ozarks. When the dam was made, this natural formation was created as the waters flooded the valley. Vintage postcard. *Courtesy Janice Tremeear.*

at the end of O Road by Millstone, the Millstone and Pistol Point are very haunted. A sad past ensures that the lost souls there are unable to find peace.

Pistol Point was readily used by the Kansas City Mafia to take care of a lot of their more morbid business, according to local lore.

Osage Indians and their one-time burial ground were disturbed by the development that took place. The souls that roam that part of the lake will never rest. History shows that the land, before Bagnell Dam made this area such a vacation paradise, was rife with turmoil, as in the case of the infamous Slicker War.

SLICKER WAR

During the 1840s, the county was beset by an organized band of counterfeiters and horse and cattle thieves. In what became known as the Slicker War, a company of regulators was raised to combat the thieves. The term "slicker" came from the form of punishment inflicted on the suspects that involved whipping them with hickory withes, or "slicking" them.

The regulators committed excesses when a few took the opportunity to settle personal grudges. The regulators were disbanded when the thieves were driven out, but animosities remained among those who were unjustly targeted. Several gangs under the name Slicker roamed Missouri in the 1800s. It's generally thought that the origin of the Slickers came from a Hatfield and McCoy–style family feud in Benton and Polk Counties.

Colonel Hiram Turk migrated with his family to Warsaw about 1839. The family had a reputation for being courteous and well-educated. Turk went about setting up a store and saloon. Warsaw was settled in 1820, when Lewis Bledsoe established a ferry across the Osage River, and was named the Benton County seat in 1838.

Andy Jones and his family moved from Kentucky to settle by the Pomme de Terre River. Counterfeiting was soon added to their repertoire of gambling and betting on horse races. On election day in 1840, Andy Jones came into Turk's store to vote. A fight broke out over politics. One of the Turk's sons pulled a knife and was charged with assault.

On the day of the trial, a witness was threatened by one of the Turks. A gunfight ensued, and Jim Turk died.

Later, Andy Jones shot and killed Hiram Turk after Hiram reported a Jones relative, who was a fugitive, to the authorities.

Townspeople became entangled in the feud. Those with the Turks "slicked" the Joneses, and the Jones family retaliated.

Many of the slicking attacks resulted in deaths; those who survived wanted to move out of the area. People who sided with the Turks were the Slickers, and those who joined with the Joneses became the Anti-Slickers. This "war" spread throughout the Ozarks. Soon, the governor was called upon to put a stop to the violence in Benton County. Now there were four armed factions fighting, and things could only get worse. Some fled into Texas and Louisiana, but the Slickers followed.

When enough of the Turks and Joneses lay dead, both of the original families moved away.

Other Slicker groups operated in St. Charles and McDonald Counties in eastern Missouri, and some small factions grew up in other areas of the state. The Slickers spread out into four surrounding states as well.

Yes, there are ghost stories in Warsaw reporting numerous sightings of Civil War soldiers from both sides strolling complacently inside the town's limits and along the shore of the lake. One phantom even bears a cannonball-sized hole in his midsection. The Bledsoe Ferry Public Use Area has a nautical ghost, an old skipper who appears menacing, yet no one knows his history or why he haunts the site of the ferry. Stranger is the lady with a knife embedded in her skull. Stranger still is that she's seen riding a horse on a highway near Warsaw.

Two more female ghosts are noted, one an elderly sorceress and the other a woman in flames. At the old cemetery, there is a woman wandering about wearing a long bloody dress.

Thirteen miles north of Warsaw, the hauntings continue with more Civil War soldiers. A dead hunter drags his kill, a moose, near Karr Lake Dam during the wee hours of the morning. This man is mangled (perhaps from his encounter with the now dead moose?), and he is the most active ghost in the area.

Timberline Lake has a shackled woman at the water's edge.

A certain Slicker group did serve a decent purpose during the lawless times in the forested Missouri Ozarks.

Sunset at Lake of the Ozarks. Postcard. *Courtesy Janice Tremeear.*

Of the three hundred vigilante groups of that time, the Lincoln County Slickers was the largest and most widely known. This mob of Slickers is second in notoriety only to the Baldknobbers of southwestern Missouri. Lincoln County's Slickers elected a "captain," wrote a constitution and bylaws and had some of the most influential men in the county as members.

A Godfather-type criminal launched his intricate syndicate long before the Mafia set foot in Kansas City or St. Louis. The Slickers brought him to his knees.

John Avy became the "Phantom of the Ozarks" with his ability to keep his true identity hidden and with the moblike organization he built during the 1830s. Avy set the standard for the Godfather figure with a gang more notorious than the James-Younger Gang. As J.W. Vincent said, "The ruling spirit was a man far removed from his assumed character of a simple pioneer. He was so shrewd in concealing his identity and his connection with the outlaws."

Avy cultivated a reputation as a mild, well-heeled man, surrounded in mystery, an enigma that hid the true, violent and perverse nature of the man. Avy chose Ha Ha Tonka Spring as his base of operations. The caves, springs, deep gorges and heavy forests perfectly hid Avy and his secret "Bank of Niangua." Years earlier, the Osage had considered the spring sacred ground, using it for tribal meetings. Once abandoned by the Indians, few men visited the wooded place.

Avy's men stole cattle and beat or killed those who tried to reclaim their lost property. Laws existed to deal with criminals, but there was not much in the way of authority to correct the situation. Avy soon brought about one of

Ha Ha Tonka Castle after the fire. Vintage photo. *Courtesy Janice Tremeear.*

the most lawless times in Missouri history: "One of Avy's henchmen smugly boasted to a settler that he could steal a horse and have the settler sent to the penitentiary for the crime."

Avy remained largely unnoticed, even with a burgeoning crime cartel. Seeking to control potential enemies Avy got his men elected into public office. He branched out into counterfeiting by establishing his fake bank and bringing printing presses into the caves at his hideout in Ha Ha Tonka, going so far as to print Mexican currency.

His fraud was discovered by accident, and the banks demanded action. A Jefferson City marshal led a posse to the spring to arrest several of Avy's men but not the mastermind himself. According to Vincent, "The organization [Slickers] had for its aim only *resistance to unlawful encroachments*."

The Slickers sprang into action in the early 1840s to defeat Avy and his mob. This group was composed of local citizens, the gangbusters of their time. The justice they meted out was unique but effective. Miscreants were stripped of their clothing and whipped in public with hickory branches that had been toughened by heating.

Avy rose to the challenge by placing spies within the ranks of the Slickers, and thus he was well informed of their activities and plans. However, his men soon became disgruntled, and Avy was in danger of having his identity exposed. He put out a murder order on the judges of the county, but his men proved less than capable. They murdered an innocent young man who happened to be in the wrong place at the wrong time.

The unfortunate young man was near the home of an Anti-Slicker, and the townspeople arrested the son of the homeowner. A mob of Slickers stormed the jail with lynching in mind. The blacksmith stood ready with his hammer to bash in the door, and a self-appointed executioner waited with his noose at the proper tree.

At the begging of the murdered boy's father, the mob agreed to let a court of law decide the boy's fate. The suspect was left in the hands of the jailer, who was also the sheriff and thought to be one of John Avy's agents.

By morning, both sheriff and the suspect were long gone, never to been seen again.

The mob under Avy's command was falling apart. The Slickers had brought about the disintegration of Avy's well-laid plans. He became a snitch on his own organization, his men and what part they played in his schemes. He had two of his men, one of them a lieutenant, set up to be murdered, luring one of his victims from his home. As Vincent notes, "Avy... turned traitor at the last in order to save his own worthless life."

Ha Ha Tonka's caves and forests couldn't hide Avy's men forever, and the Slickers rounded up many of his men. Those who escaped were disillusioned with their leader and fled. Many of Avy's men were allowed to leave the region, and those who claimed they were Avy's victims remained under probation, with the Slickers keeping watch.

A raid on the caves of Ha Ha Tonka failed to turn up much evidence on the Bank of Niangua, but the presses and equipment were located nearby. Unfortunately, history gets fuzzy at this point. It's thought that Avy confessed and was exiled from the state of Missouri.

At last, the decade of lawlessness ended, but the reputation of the Slickers remained. Justice had a new meaning—mob rule—with vigilantes spreading law without due process. Vincent writes:

> *Thrown upon their own resources in the inhospitable wilderness, beyond the reach of the protecting arm of the law, confronted by an enemy more unscrupulous, cunning and insinuating than the red savage of the forest, they opposed force with force.*
>
> *Of course, the immediate effect of the "Slicker" victory was a general purification of the moral atmosphere. Crude and primitive as had been the remedies employed, the cure was radical, and for a time complete.*

In three years' time, the Slickers ended their rule of Lincoln County after many men were killed or expelled from the group. Missouri stung from the effects of the Slickers, Anti-Slickers and lawlessness of that time period. Some of the spirits now seen aimless and lost and could well belong to the men who lost their lives before the Lake of the Ozarks adopted the "wholesome family atmosphere" that exists there today. As Vincent predicted, "No more counterfeiting, no more horse stealing, no more insecurity and dread of unseen evil."

HA HA TONKA STATE PARK

Native Americans were drawn to the Niangua River and countryside by their beauty. Daniel and Nathan Boone trapped for fur here. Zebulon Pike passed through on his exploration of the West. Settlers were awed by the sight of what is now Ha Ha Tonka State Park. Herbert S. Hadley, governor of Missouri in 1909, proposed the first state park here, but it did not become a reality until 1978.

Ha Ha Tonka has a number of unique geological features. A 60-foot natural bridge, 70 feet wide, sits 100 feet in the air. Whispering Dell sink basin is 150 feet deep. Two bluff caves, Counterfeiter's Cave and Robber's Cave, sheltered criminals in the 1860s, and one has the tale of a ghost lingering about. The Coliseum is a steep sinkhole 500 feet long and 300 feet wide.

Ha Ha Tonka's 250-foot-tall bluffs shadow the spring. This spring is Missouri's twelfth largest, and forty-eight million gallons of water flow daily from underground. The spring spews from the mouth of an existing cavern still being eroded and carved by the force of the water.

Trails and boardwalks make it easy for visitors to experience the honeycomb of tunnels, caverns, springs and sinkholes. Visitors can peer into caves, trek through and around sinkholes or climb from the spring to the castle on wooden steps that circle the spring chasm. A visitors' center features a large relief map of the park carved from stone.

Ha Ha Tonka State Park contains one of Missouri's best examples of a woodland landscape. Woodlands are areas that are neither totally forest nor totally prairie, where prairie grasses such as little bluestem and Indian grass flourish in open forests of post oak, blackjack oak, black hickory and white oak. More than four hundred species of plants have been recorded here.

Wildflower displays change throughout the summer. Ha Ha Tonka Oak Woodland Natural Area is protected, and a short self-guiding nature trail, as well as a seven-mile backpack trail, allows visitors to experience this rich woodland landscape.

Missouri's "deserts" are the large glades containing plants and animals more often associated with the southwestern United States. Glade inhabitants include the large yellow-flowered Missouri evening primrose, the Missouri brown-eyed Susan, prairie scorpions and the Missouri tarantula.

Ha Ha Tonka Castle

One of Missouri's castles perches like a predatory bird high atop a bluff overlooking Ha Ha Tonka Spring and Lake of the Ozarks. The castle itself is not haunted, but objects once residing within its stone walls might be.

Ha Ha Tonka is an Osage Indian name for a region of rugged scenic beauty in the Missouri Ozarks and the site of a European-style mansion known as Ha Ha Tonka Castle.

In 1905, a self-made Kansas City businessman, Robert McClure Snyder, began construction of his dream home atop a 250-foot cliff overlooking Big Spring, a natural spring in the south central Missouri Ozarks.

Outside of Camdenton, the region is known as Ha Ha Tonka, or Hahatonka, and is most often translated as the "Land of the Laughing Water" because of the sound the water makes at the base of the cliff.

Robert M. Snyder visited the site in 1903. He was so impressed by the site that he eventually purchased more than five thousand acres. He had stopped at a hotel in Lebanon, Missouri, where the owner told him about an area he co-owned. Snyder took up the owner's suggestion and made the twenty-five-mile journey via horse and buggy to Ha Ha Tonka.

He saw a landscape and natural resources that the American Indians had loved for centuries: the abundance of wild game and waterfowl, fish swimming in the clear streams and sites for camping in the villages or caves along the Niangua and Osage Rivers. He saw the topography known as karst, including underground streams, springs, cliffs, sinkholes, caves, chasms and natural rock formations that had been forming since prehistoric times. And he wanted to preserve all of it.

Envisioning a private retreat with a European-style castle, Snyder's plans included a center atrium rising three and a half stories to a skylight. A central hallway rose to the height of the building. An enormous eighty-foot-tall water tower, a stone stable and nine greenhouses were ultimately constructed on the estate. The stone and timber originated locally. The actual construction began in 1905.

At the time of Robert Snyder's first visit to the region, Ha Ha Tonka contained several buildings, including a school, a gristmill and a hotel. He made his first purchase of land at Ha Ha Tonka Park in 1904. He continued buying land until he had sixty adjoining tracts equaling fifty-four hundred acres.

By March 1905, he came with a corps of engineers and landscape architects to locate the grounds for his new home, to plan walkways and drives and to use an already-existing dam and old mill site for electricity and elevating water to the top of the cliff.

The cost of construction of the stone mansion would be approximately $40,000, and it would have sixty rooms. Cement was hauled from Lebanon, twenty-five miles away. Lumber was ordered from a nearby sawmill in Decaturville. The growing number of workmen created an increased demand for lodging and board.

The hotel was used to house the labor force. A cottage was renovated and used as a temporary residence for Snyder and his wife. A tool house and workshop were built on the cliff, and excavation of the stone and rock was underway.

Robert and his family spent most of the summer of 1905 in Europe. While away, a telephone system was installed in the park. Heavy blasting was heard for miles.

The eighty-foot-high water tower was built to force water up to the mansion by gravity from the spring at the base of the cliff. Progress continued on building roads that did not detract from the natural scenery. When the Snyders returned, a new steam sawmill was in use for lumber.

The first railroad at Ha Ha Tonka carried stone from the quarries up the cliff to the mansion, and stone masons were added to the workforce. A boat was used as a ferry to transport lumber across the lake. By September 1906, the mansion had a roof and a large fountain in front. The landscape architect was from England, and an interior designer was brought in from New York. Workmen shifted their attention to building the greenhouses and stables.

Robert Snyder's untimely death in one of the state's first automobile accidents, in Kansas City on October 27, 1906, halted the castle's construction.

Snyder was one of the first people to own a car, and his chauffeur was driving down Independence Avenue with Snyder in the backseat. When a small boy ran out in front of the car, the chauffeur swerved, but the boy was hit and died. Snyder was thrown out of the car and died instantly.

The castle found new life after Snyder's three sons, Robert Jr., Leroy and Kenneth, finished building their father's dream. The roof was finished first for protection, but the interior was not completed until 1922.

Not quite as elaborate as originally planned, the property was leased to a woman for use as a hotel, until tragedy struck in 1942. The entire interior was gutted by fire when sparks from a chimney ignited the roof. The carriage house burned the same day. Now the castle crouches stark and blackened against the lush landscape.

In 1976, vandals burned the water tower. Today, only ruins remain.

The enormous effort of building the castle strikes all who visit the ruins. In a virtual wilderness during the early twentieth century, the challenges of such an undertaking are awe-inspiring. Robert Snyder owned the Snyder Gas Company in Kansas City, and he engaged the architect Adrian Van Brunt for the castle's design. A Scottish foreman was brought in to ensure proper European authenticity of the building. After Snyder's death, the pace of construction slowed, and the castle was completed in 1922. Soon after, the family business slid into decline.

After the death of his father, Robert Jr. lived at the castle and suffered health problems. Interested in history, both local and regional, he amassed quite a library of rare books. Over one thousand volumes made up the most

Above: Ha Ha Tonka Castle ruins in Ha Ha Tonka State Park, near Lake of the Ozarks. *Photo by Dave Harkins.*

Below: Ha Ha Tonka Castle (before the fire). Vintage photo. *Courtesy Janice Tremeear.*

extensive collection of works on regional history, literature and folklore. Robert kept his beloved books at the castle.

By the time of the Depression, the Snyder fortune had been depleted by the litigation over Bagnell Dam, and the castle was converted into a lodge. The books were donated to the University of Kansas City and missed the destruction of the fire of 1942.

When the university became UMKC (University of Missouri–Kansas City), the Snyder books were housed in closed stacks in the general library. Kept in a separate room with a full-time librarian, the books were carefully catalogued.

Odd things are known to happen within this quiet bastion of learning. Feelings of being watched are present, and books that are left lying open to certain pages are found to be displaying a different page upon the librarian's return, even when the pages are held down by paperweights.

Rustling pages are heard, as are the sounds of books being pulled off the shelves when no one is present. Perhaps the spirit of Robert M. Snyder Jr. remains with his beloved collection.

The Ha Ha Tonka ruins attract thousands of visitors each year. They stand as a reminder of one man's vision and of fortunes lost. Robert Jr.'s love of Missouri history remains strong, and his collection allows us to touch for a brief moment the strength of a family's comment to following a dream.

In 1978, the State of Missouri bought the estate and opened it to the public as a state park. Ha Ha Tonka is about five miles southwest of Camdenton and covers approximately twenty-four hundred acres on the Niangua Arm of the Lake of the Ozarks.

The castle and perhaps Robert Jr.'s books give us a link between this world and the next as we view the efforts that meant so much to one family.

MILLER COUNTY

If a tree is struck by lightning, the wood must never be used for fuel.
—Indian lore

It is bad luck to lay a hat on a bed.
—Ozark superstition

IBERIA ACADEMY

Miller County is home to a town with a rare name. Iberia is not often found; indeed, the only other city in the United States with a similar name is New Iberia, Louisiana. Iberia is a Celtic word whose meaning has been lost. Iberia is also a peninsula of southwest Europe occupied by Spain and Portugal. Its ancient inhabitants are likely the source of the name. The Greeks called these peoples Iberians (probably after Ebro, or the Iberus, River, the second longest river on the peninsula).

To the northeast are the Pyrenees, and to the south is Gibraltar, a narrow strait separating the land from North Africa. Bordering the eastern coast is the Atlantic Ocean, with the Mediterranean Sea on the north and west coasts. Iberia is the most westerly point of continental Europe and includes Cape da Roca in Portugal.

The Celtic culture spread to the Iberian Peninsula and formed two tribes, the Hispano-Celtic class and the Celtiberian, who came via France and intermingled with the people of the Ebro Valley and Spain.

The Iberia we're referring to in this book is in America's Vacation Land, near the Lake of the Ozarks, and was once the home of the Osage Indians and a man named George White Bear, who lived alongside the white man once settlers came to build homes.

This first post office was constructed next to Rabbit Head Creek on a site later dubbed Oakhurst. Oakhurst occupied the Old Herald Water Mill Road leading to Camden County (formerly Kinderhook County). William Lennox operated a trading post that fell to destruction during the Civil War and was never rebuilt.

Iberia was platted in 1859 by Henry M. Dickerson, who owned all the land. St. Louis Street was one of the two streets he laid out, running north and south at a width of sixty feet. Main Street ran east and west and was seventy feet wide.

During the early years of the Civil War, a fort was constructed to prevent marauders. This became a command post for the militia under the leadership of Captain William Long. On August 29, 1862, Captain Long led Company G, Enrolled Militia, into a skirmish about four miles east of Iberia. They met Colonel Robert R. Lawther's Rebels, a company of about 125 men. Long's troops numbered 40 enlisted men, with 2 lieutenants. Greatly outnumbered, Long suffered the loss of 1 man, with several wounded, and the Confederates lost 1 man, with 3 of the many wounded taken prisoner.

The citizens of Iberia were divided in their loyalties, and bushwhackers murdered Captain Long at his parents' home. Long aided his parents and an elderly slave to escape the ruffians and partook in a gun battle with them. They set fire to the home and shot William as he exited the burning house.

Iberia bears the nickname "Rock Town" from a tall tale that says that during a skirmish at the fort, the opposing forces ran out of ammunition and took up throwing rocks at each other in anger. A more likely version says that a young black man who voted for Abraham Lincoln (and thus carried the title Republican) walked into town with his ox cart of grist for the mill. He carried rocks between the barrels, and when ruffians in the town accosted him, the young man aimed an accurate throw and knocked the vandal to the ground. When others came to aid the ruffian, the young man continued to throw his rocks and held off the crowd.

Iberia Academy opened its doors to eighteen eighth-grade students on October 1, 1890. One high school student joined the younger classmates in the one-room building.

Situated nearly dead center in Iberia is the rambling academy campus, four buildings sitting at odd angles within a triangle of 2.66 acres. The oldest structure is the President's Home, believed to have been constructed about 1909. Other buildings are the women's dormitory, the administration building and gym and the old slaves' quarters. Part of the haunting here is concerned with the man who once lived in the slaves' quarters. John lived with his wife in the 1830 cabin, later remodeled and expanded in 1890. At this writing, only the main building is still safe to enter. The others are unsafe or torn down. A rock wall marks the campus boundaries with a stone gateway set at the east end of the triangle. A large stone monument stands inside the gate, towering nearly ten feet in height.

On April 23, 1891, the articles of Miller County, written and signed by citizens of Missouri, stated, "The name of this institution shall be called Iberia Academy."

Two years earlier, George Byron Smith and Mabel White had married and ventured out into the world. On a train in Illinois, George met a traveling salesman, who told him of a place in the Ozark Mountains with "some little cabins, some old women smokin' corncob pipes and some grown men playin' marbles to help them forgit they're alive." He told George that when he saw those signs, he'd know he had reached Iberia, Missouri.

The newly married Smiths began their school in the fall of 1890. The people of Iberia were very poor in the late nineteenth century, so low tuition was established for the school. A full term cost six dollars at the academy while the common school's fees were three dollars for the primary department, four dollars for intermediate and five dollars for the advanced students. Room and board was available for two dollars per week. In 1910, tuition increased to nine dollars yearly. Board in the Ladies' Hall was one dollar and eighty-five cents per week. Rooms in town could be found for students at fifteen cents a week.

The girls' dorm was the second building constructed on the land. Called "Girls' Cottage," it was a six-room house for the young ladies who boarded at the school.

The gym was built in 1926, christened the Martin Gymnasium in honor of Charles Martin of Webster Groves, Missouri. It was built by the students who were learning stonemasonry of native stone cut from the academy's quarry.

Once the Adda Danforth Weaving Cabin, the original building was the first on campus and was occupied by a black family. The house, along with three and a half acres of land, was purchased and added to the academy's campus. The girls attending school remembered the log cabin fondly as "Home Sweet Home," where the laundry was done. A donation in 1926 allowed for reconstruction of the cabin and the naming of the home after the donor's (W.H. Danforth's) wife. A room was added in 1937 from log that had been part of the first building erected in the community.

The weaving cabin at one time held the post office and had a portion of the house for the family and a section set aside for the slaves. It was later divided into five rooms for weaving. The girls of the school created rugs, curtains, purses, scarves, ties, bags and table runners—all items for sale for the school.

There are ghosts associated with the cabin and a sad tale indeed of what happened there.

As the tale unfolds, the master of the land was taking advantage of John's wife. In retribution, John "took advantage" of the master's wife, and the act resulted in her pregnancy. The master caught John and his wife together and killed his wife and unborn child, John and John's wife.

It is said that John remains nearby because of his lost child and due to fear of what "awaits him on the other side."

At the Iberia Academy, there were several deaths on the property, most from disease. There are many grave sites on the property as well.

Mabel White Smith died at the academy in 1932 in her home; her husband, of advanced age, retired reluctantly and return to his home in Princeton, Illinois.

Freddy Bee is the current owner. He says there are "orbs constantly on the move." Neighbors walking past the empty building have asked him, "Who are the people looking out the academy windows?"

A room that Bee's daughter occupied as a bedroom has the most activity. His daughter said that while staying in that room, she was visited by ghosts on a nightly basis.

Dave Harkins and his team, TOPS, investigated Iberia Academy and came away with several EVPs and photos showing glowing anomalies. One is thought to be of a little girl looking out the doorway at the old slave house. I visited with Dave, along with Ali, Andrew and Charlene Wells of Route 66 Paranormal Alliance. We sat with Dave and a TOPS team member, RoseAnna O'Dell, in Dave's home near Lebanon, Missouri. Dave showed us photos taken throughout the night he and his team spent at the Iberia Academy. He told us that "school girls died of cholera." He offered the following version of John's story: "The slave owner killed his wife and mulatto baby, slave father, his wife and committed suicide."

COOPER COUNTY

When the crow is on the fence,
Rain will come hence.
When the crow is on the ground,
Rain will come down.
—Ozark superstition

A white Christmas foretells a lean graveyard.
—Ozarks superstition

RAVENSWOOD MANSION, BOONVILLE

If you're looking for a mansion that bears the mystery of a castlelike dwelling out of a movie, then Ravenswood may be up your alley. One would fully expect to find the secret passageways and hidden chambers of a mystery movie or treasure stashed within the walls or buried out on the grounds.

Between Bunceton and Pilot Grove in Cooper County sits a dream of antiquity.

In 1804, Lewis and Clark reported saltwater springs in the area that now comprises Howard, Cooper and Saline Counties. The largest salt spring was the Boone's Lick. The area around this spring was ideal for settlement, and Boone's Lick Country was a primary destination for pioneers moving west.

Nathan and Daniel Morgan Boone, sons of famous frontiersman Daniel Boone, went into partnership with James and Jesse Morrison in 1805.

They produced salt from brine water poured into iron kettles and heated to boiling on a stone furnace. Salt crystallized in the bottom of the kettle as the water evaporated.

They shipped the salt via keelboat on the Missouri River to St. Louis. Salt, which was indispensable at the time for preserving meat and tanning hides, was produced at the site until about 1833.

As the Boonslick (the name we now use) drew settlers west, the Nelson family took interest in the beauty of the land in the 1800s.

Nadine Nelson Leonard and Charles Leonard built a home that would become the showcase of the Boonville region. Nadine came from a wealthy family in the St. Charles/St. Louis area. Her father asked her where she wanted a home built, in town (Boonville) or out in the country. She chose the country, knowing he would build a second home to have her close to him.

I spoke with Jamey Leonard, a direct descendant of the family who has owned the mansion for six generations. "The Leonards were the social icons of Boonville," Jamey says. "Nadine built the home to show off their wealth."

The home is like a time capsule; period clothing from around the world still hangs in the wardrobes, dishes sit in the cupboards and records and journals of the working farm's daily life are lying about. All the items the first generation acquired make the home quite the museum piece. Over thirty rooms are furnished exactly as they were when occupied by Jamey's ancestors. Ravenswood is located between Bunceton and Pilot Grove in Cooper County, just outside Booneville.

Slaves were owned on the property, with house slaves named Glen and Hortense, and it's said that the family always treated their slaves with respect. There are several slave graves located on the mansion's grounds; many of these, sadly, are unmarked, making it difficult for descendants to trace their family history. This was probably not an uncommon practice in the 1800s for slave owners. I grew up on a farm in Montgomery County, Missouri. Our deed stated that the farm had slaves, and we had a small cabin we thought might have been one of the (or the only) slave houses, but there were no details on the slaves.

I found a report on the tombstone that Nadine constructed. She outlived her husband and built the mausoleum underground with a large monument featuring a young woman leaning against the stone tablet. This was in keeping with the use of female figures on gravestones as allegories. A well-established tradition, the practice of portraying females on headstones came about in the 1920s.

Early on, women were restricted in home and social life. Their greatest potential was through reproduction and the rearing of the children. Females in grave art stood for the values of purity and virtue as defined by the limited Victorian worldview on the standard allowed to women.

Young women in particular were adulated because they carried the greatest potential for reproduction. A popular female figure was the Gibson girl, always young and virtuous but a little flirtatious as well. In real life, woman's role was severely limited, yet she was allegorized as an ethereal creature. The late nineteenth and early twentieth centuries saw a change in women's roles in the home and society, and this was reflected in graveyard art.

Margaret Nelson Stephens (Nadine's sister) erected the last female figure in the Boonslick area in 1923. The figure is of a mature woman, not a young idealized female.

Nadine Leonard died in her room, and her body was removed and taken to Boonville for burial. When the family returned, they found her bedroom door locked from the inside. Jamey's grandfather was a teenager at the time and witnessed the event. Jamey says his grandfather "climbed in through the window to unlock the door. It was jammed and remained that way for days. When the door was about to be taken off its hinges, it unlocked."

Jamey lost an uncle on the estate as well when the man's parked car clicked into neutral, rolled back and smashed him against the gates he was trying to open.

Members of Jamey's family have heard the sounds of breaking glass downstairs yet nothing is broken or disturbed when they check. A farmhand saw Jamey's grandmother at the top of the stairs watching him, but the woman had died three years earlier. A disembodied voice once answered, "Not enough" when Jamey asked, "How many beers did you have?"

Jamey's mother was giving a tour of the house and had been sitting on the couch. She got up and left the room. Upon returning, the pillows had been tossed about, one on the floor, another in the grand hallway and one in an oriental chair.

Orbs are seen floating out of Nadine's room and into another.

There is an unsolved murder connected with the property in the 1920s. A farmhand came home from the field one day to find his wife missing. After searching, he discovered her decapitated body in the barn. He reported her death to the police and became their prime suspect. He was tried for the murder and acquitted, with the evidence showing that he did not have enough time to commit the deed.

There are reports of bumps and noises at night in the mansion, but the house is big and old and eerie, and old buildings seem to have lives of their own.

Jamey said that one night friends of his were inside the house. Loud screaming was heard, and the friends came running out, telling everyone that they'd heard pounding on the door and opened it, and no one was there. To be fair, this may have been the result of a party bonfire gone over the edge, but one never knows. Even in the family cemetery, a mere three hundred yards away and visible from the house, orbs are photographed. Most paranormal investigators discount orbs, but Jamey notes that the orbs appear in one photo and none preceding or following.

Ravenswood Mansion is open for walking tours, and visitors can roam the rooms filled with artifacts from an age long past and perhaps still be visited by the previous owners.

Overton Bottoms Conservation Area

It is bad luck to tease a "Devil's horse" or praying mantis.

The wren was declared a symbol of supernatural evil, possessed of a poisonous bite should humans attempt to harm it.

—Ozarks superstitions

The Missouri Department of Conservation once managed the Overton Bottoms Conservation Area. Now it's in the hands of the U.S. Fish and Wildlife Service. Interstate 70 runs just north of the wetlands. The bluffs and train track lay south.

I sat in our vehicle with my daughter Charlene and Ken Brewer, another of Route 66 Paranormal Alliance's team members, and gazed out over the protected wildlife refuge. Behind us was our goal for the weekend: the retreat called Ozark Avalon. Alicia Holder and Andrew Muller took us to see this area before heading back past the train tracks and the cliff cave beneath Avalon's land.

The Overton Bottoms South Unit is the largest unit of the refuge, consisting of small crop fields adjacent to open fields with a mixture of grasses and forbs. Additionally, there are large areas of dense young forests of cottonwood, silver maple, willow and box elder. A narrow strip of mature cottonwood trees grows along the river.

Seasonal wetlands exist during heavy rainfall periods or high river flows. There are scour-hole lakes, or "blowholes," remaining from previous flood events. Blowholes are bodies of water created by the raging floods of 1993 and 1995, when water scored out depressions in the flood plain, some over fifty feet deep. These scour holes contain a wide variety of fish, including largemouth bass, crappie, gar and catfish. Fishing in the blowholes can be very good, and waterfowl are attracted to the lakes.

OZARK AVALON

Located on the bluffs overlooking the Missouri River Ozark Avalon retreat is a 150-acre nature preserve. Groves, woods, meadows, a three-acre lake for swimming, an established sweat lodge, hiking trails and many natural shrines are found here. I was told that the Indians came here to gather peacefully, the land holding great significance for them.

On the property are several spots for camping, with kitchen and bathroom facilities in Avalon House. A mobile home serves as a classroom, the aptly named Frog Bog offers solar-heated showers and compost toilet areas are available. Avalon is also one of the few locations to offer green burials, with fourteen acres set aside for a graveyard.

On our weekend there, I appeared to hold a tremendous fascination for the guineas that kept stalking me. Then there was the peacock. Both days at Avalon, the peacock greeted me, slowly stepping around me. On Saturday, he serenaded me with a gooselike honking—I had no idea peacocks honked. I think perhaps the peacock and the guineas were trying to tell me something. Maybe I have a couple of new animal spirit guides.

On behalf of the gorgeous peacock, I went to my local New Age store and bought an animal totem medallion to carry with me. If I could only decipher the peacock's squawk…

The main house at Avalon is a 160-year-old, two-story home offering hostel-style sleeping space, and it comes fully equipped with ghosts.

The following report is from Alicia Holder. Alicia is one of the founders of Route 66 Paranormal Alliance:

> *I talked to Susan Stoddard, Bob James and Ed and Kristy Rupkey. Located on the bluffs above the Missouri River Valley, they are about 12 miles from Boonville and 18 miles from Columbia, Missouri. Ozark Avalon is an over 160-year-old farmhouse. The Overton Bottoms Conservation Area, south side, surrounds the property. There is a small body of water on the land that the church calls Lake Gaia, but there is no other known name for the lake.*

But the story goes back much before the home was ever there. During work on the property, relics were found, and a team of archaeologists for the local university came out and did a dig. They came to believe the land had been a place of great importance to many Indians tribes. It was a place where these tribes would gather to trade and have festivals with each other.

Many people have claimed to see Indians among the trees or feel something watching them as they walk around the land.

One of the church's parishioners, Ed, told me a story about some experiences he had of an old Indian medicine woman. He told me he has seen her many times and has had her come to him in his dreams.

Others had done something to the land, and he told me that's when she came to him in the dream. She instructed him to undo what they had done—that the spirits did not like what had been done. He did as she wished.

The farm was a working farm for many years; cows and corn were the major income. The home and land were handed down from one family member to another.

There was a story of a woman who lived there. Some believe it to be the daughter of the man who first built the home. She and her husband are just two of the spirits that have been seen. They inherited the home and land and lived there until they passed. Anyhow, she had felt ill and was bound to a wheelchair.

She was so ill for so long that they had to hire help to keep the farm going.

She is still seen to this very day sitting in her wheelchair, watching over everything going on. She has been seen on the stairs on the balcony and just off the porch of the home.

When I spoke with Susan, she told me about a dream she has had over the years about this woman. She said that in the dream she was old and would talk and just go on like an old women would, talking about work needing to be done or about things that were being done to the place.

Both stories were alike in that when they did what the spirit wanted, they felt that they made the spirits happy.

Now, as for the old man, well, I have a story about him. I was there for some R&R and was not looking to find anything. But it seemed he wanted me to know he was there. As soon as I put my things down in the room, I would be staying in that night. I felt it!

He let me know that he was there, and I said, "Don't want any thing to do with you. I'm not here for this, sorry."

Ozark Avalon Main House, a spiritual retreat located between Columbia and Boonville, Missouri. *Photo by Alicia Holder.*

I could tell this upset him. I went on my way.

Later that night, as I was talking to the others that lived there on the land about what I had felt, I was told that I was right—that there was believed to be an old man spirit there and that something had happened that had pissed him off as of late.

After my stay, when I was getting ready to go, I found my phone covered in a clear slimy film. I have never seen any thing like it, ever!

There are many tales of spirits and things seen around the land, home and old barn. Like dark phantoms. Floating specks of light. The land is open for camping and gathering to this day.

According to some of the accounts I've read, among the many Osage beliefs is that of little people. Supernatural spirits. Most cultures have these wee ones who are mischievous jokers or pranksters but offer no real harm.

This is not true for the Osage Little People, all of whom were Osage Indians who died without paint and without honor. They were the *mialuschka*, the lost souls.

Osage Little People are treated with respect and fear because, unlike friendly spirits, they are vindictive, dangerous and even deadly.

They wander the earth hungry, full of hatred for their unsettled state, and want nothing more than to add to their ranks from among those they consider prey. This would include any who desecrate their holy lands.

The Osage Little People at times might be content merely playing a prank or frightening their prey. They might spoil food or chase a skunk into a home. But their pranks could quickly become deadly—trees falling on a windless day or rocks falling down from a cliff with no creatures present. Should the little people get very angry, their prey would have to get a blessing from a shaman, with no guarantee that this could turn aside their wrath.

Oddly enough, only an Osage shaman can sense the presence of the little people.

The little people might be seen as Indians dressed in native costumes, with hair shaved into Mohawks, blankets wrapped around them and faces without paint. They have dead eyes, burning with the light of night.

Sometimes the little people aren't seen as people, but they're still about. They have another guise—that of a bird. An owl to be exact. You know they're there when you see them looking at you, when you've been spotted as prey or when you hear the owl's song.

The little people of the Osage are reputed to be ugly, wrinkled and gnomelike, wearing tattered, old-fashioned clothes. They are kidnappers who trade babies for changelings and are rumored to be warriors who died without honor.

There are digs that have unearthed the bodies of people of short stature. In Wyoming, a race of small people called the Nimerigar was uncovered. When these people were too old or ill to be of use to their society, they were killed with a blow to the head. A fourteen-inch mummy was found in 1932 in the San Pedro Mountains. Some theories claim that the mummy was a child; others say it was a sixty-five-year-old man. The San Pedro Mummy findings proving it was a man disappeared, however. Other burial sites containing a pygmy race have been located near Cochocton, Ohio (three-foot-tall people), and in 1876 a site was discovered in Coffee County, Tennessee, that covered six acres, holding the remains of thousands of dwarf-sized people.

Interestingly enough, north of the Ozark Avalon retreat and I-70 is a small town called Rocheport, where the Rocheport Cemetery was part of the set for Stephen King's movie *Pet Cemetery*, and the famous Missouri, Kansas and Texas Railroad (MKT) tunnel was used for filming Stephen King's *Sometimes They Come Back*. This tunnel is the only one on the MKT Railroad.

Rocheport itself stands much as it once did 140 years ago. Remnants of times past abound in the historic village. Stories of Native Americans, the

Louisiana Territory and Lewis and Clark have been passed down through family lines.

Riverboats navigated the Missouri. A grand political convention was held. Vicious Confederate guerillas seized the town, and scandalous goings-on surrounded the construction of the Rocheport Tunnel. Citizens enjoyed "moonlight excursions" on the river, and spectators watched the locomotives roar past on the MKT line.

The tunnel's entrance is rough rock, but the interior is hand-hewn brick over one hundred years old. The other side is cut stone, and the entire work is impressive in its stability. The hill the tunnel bores through was very well known during the 1800s and was featured in Lewis and Clark's journals. It was called Manitou Bluff because of the huge cave drawings painted on the sides of the limestone cliffs.

Rocheport was known as the "Mouth of the Moniteau," and Moniteau Creek was known as the "Creek of the Great Spirit." Moniteau is the French spelling of *Manitou*, the Algonquian word for "Great Spirit," a supernatural power that permeates the world, a power inherent in natural phenomena (animals, plants, weather, geographical features) and possessed in varying degrees by both spiritual and human beings. Manitou are personified as spirit-beings interacting with humans and one another, led by the Great Manitou (Kitchi-Manitou).

Throughout the late seventeenth century and until the early nineteenth century, the indigenous peoples inhabiting the middle section of what is now Missouri were the native tribes of the Osage, Kansas, Iowa, Sac and Fox. They were hunter-gathers and raised many crops.

Thomas Jefferson purchased the Louisiana Territory in 1803 from Napoleon with the idea of setting aside the land as Indian Territory. But his good intentions failed when the early settlers did not give up their claims to the land they staked out. In 1808 and 1825, the Osage signed treaties to cede their lands, which included all of Missouri.

As Rocheport grew into an important river town for shipping goods, it became more and more unruly, with citizens and visitors alike partaking in distilled spirits and getting into drunken rows.

The Ozark Avalon retreat sits within the Manitou Bluffs Region. Extending fifty-five river miles, this area covers the Missouri River from Jefferson City to Boonville. Lewis and Clark recorded the pictograph painted by Native Americans on the limestone bluffs bordering the river in June 1804. The mysterious Indian painters may have been the Osage, since they were a very spiritual people and are identified with other pictographs in the area.

The Manitou was a humanlike figure with what looked to be antlers emerging from the head. The bluffs were covered with mysterious and undecipherable symbols and images.

Excited by the pictographs, the Americans, French and other European travelers speculated that the drawings represented spiritual concepts held sacred by the unknown Native American artists who drew them, particularly those containing the Manitou. These painting were placed high above the ground, accessible by inching along narrow rock ledges.

Observers concluded that the marked cliffs indicated places particularly favored by a higher spiritual being (the Manitou) and infused with sacred powers. The following journal entry was written by William Clark on June 7, 1804:

A Short distance above the mouth of this Creek, is Several Courious Paintings and Carveing in the projecting rock of Limestone inlade with white red & blue flint, of a verry good quality, the Indians have taken of this flint great quantities. We landed at this Inscription and found it a Den of rattle Snakes, we had not landed 3 minutes before three verry large Snakes wer observed on the Crevises of the rocks & killed.

One other expedition brought the following report by Sergeant John Ordway: "We passed a high cliff of Rocks on which was painted the Pickture of the Deavel."

Prince Maximilian was also intrigued by the pictographs and in 1883 journeyed to the west with artist Karl Bodmer. Maximilian wrote:

Just before dinner we reached Rockport (Rocheport), a village founded two years ago on the Manito (Monitueau) River. Near this place there are again many red figures on the rocky wall, among others that of a man with uplifted arms.

Unfortunately, in the 1900s, railroad men cutting a hole into the hill that stood in their way did not see the pictographs or did not care about the spiritual symbols overlooking Rocheport. Dynamite and pickaxes tore into the hillside, taking away rock and the best of the Manitou pictographs.

In keeping with the idea of the Osage's belief in the little people tormenting those who desecrated the land upon which the Manitou paintings were placed is the possibility of the haunting of the land beneath Ozark Avalon. Odd things happen on the property and in the main house. Shadows drop from trees on either side of the snakelike driveway. Something dark is seen in the upstairs section of the barn. Even during the Midwest's version of the Burning Man Festival, when the entire open flatland on the ridge is full of campers, strange occurrences happen that cannot be explained.

The woman who haunts the main house is reported in two forms—that of a younger woman and that of an older, frail lady who sits in her wheelchair.

I was drawn to the beautiful wooden staircase inside the home's entryway. The people who stay in the house year-round said that the little girls who live there have seen the female ghost on the balcony at the top of the stairs.

Apparently, the grounds attract entities, too. We stayed overnight in another home on the property with a history of a dark apparition coming into one of the guest rooms to harass anyone sleeping there. After dinner, Andrew went out onto the back deck and took a few pictures. I-70 is clearly seen from the back of the house, and a line of trees grows along the edge of the property before is slopes down to the bluffs separating Avalon from the wildlife preserve.

Andrew came back inside telling us that the photos were odd. Only one tree showed up in the pictures, and the others were blackened out by darkness. The porch light did not reach beyond the deck railing more than a few inches. Ali went outside to see for herself and then came back indoors. "That is the blackest darkness I've ever seen," she said. I went for a flashlight and took a look for myself. The porch light was on. Andrew came out and showed me the large cedar tree that was the only one showing up in his photos. The line of trees wasn't visible, yet I could see the lights of the vehicles to the north on Highway 70.

My flashlight failed to illuminate the yard beyond just a few inches past the deck. This lasted for a few minutes, and before Andrew or I could walk out into the yard, everything brightened. The light illuminated the yard all the way back to the line of trees, which were now clearly visible.

About 2:00 a.m., I finally went to bed in the room with the entity that attacks sleeping people. Charlene and I were sharing a bed in that guestroom. Ali and Andrew had an air mattress in the second guest bedroom, and Ken was in the living room on the couch. Charlene went to bed earlier since she was driving home the next day. No sooner did I lie down than I felt something bouncing on the bed near my legs. I looked, and nothing was there. I lay down again and once more felt the bouncing on the bed. After that stopped, I fell asleep, but periodically during the night, the top blanket slid off on my side of the bed. I would sit up and straighten the blanket, not thinking much about it.

In the morning, Charlene asked me if I'd heard the man pacing about in the room. Apparently, every time I moved, the pacing stopped. Ali and

Andrew experienced the same pacing coming from the closet in their room and described a man in a hat. In researching this figure, I found that he, or his cohorts, has been seen frequently around the country.

Reports of the "Hatman" have been on the increase. He is always dark, a shadow form—tall and thin—and sometimes his face can be seen. More often than not, he is merely a shadow man, but he always wears a wide-brimmed hat, and those who encounter him have a feeling of unease. Some people call him the "Watcher."

I didn't hear a thing, but I was the only one who felt someone or something on my bed. It makes me wonder if we experienced a visit from the Hatman or if one of the little people was playing a prank on us.

Other tribes also held legends of little people—the Maha, Sioux, Cherokee, Oto, Yakama, Mohegan-Pequot, Ute and Iroquois, to name a few.

COLE COUNTY

Burdock root, when strung like beads, was believed to protect children from witches.
—Ozark superstition

JEFFERSON CITY

Missouri's state capital is haunted, if you believe the legend handed down from 1993, when a repairman working in the attic saw an eight-year-old girl playing nearby. She wore a white dress and lingered in the attic most of the day. When he reported the child, he was told that no little girl was present. A search proved that no children were on the grounds at that time. This was during Christopher Bond's term as governor, and the Bonds didn't have a daughter.

The child is assumed to be Carrie, the daughter of Governor Thomas Crittenden. Carrie died in 1883 of diphtheria, as did many children of that time. Crittenden is remembered for his stand against bandits and marauding guerillas, and he set into motion the events leading up to the death of Jesse James.

Kidnappers threatened to take Carrie while Crittenden struggled to put a halt to bandit activity, and he posted bodyguards. But for all his power and care, he couldn't stop disease from taking his daughter. Carrie has not been reported inside the mansion since that first sighting. There are other occurrences, however. Objects move, and candles melt down to a puddle of wax moments after being lit. Laughter is heard, and the elevator travels on its own.

Other people died in the mansion, though Carrie was the first. Mrs. Alexander Dockery was semi invalid when she arrived at the mansion, but she continued to be active. The former Mary Elizabeth Bird died on January 1, 1093. Governor John Sappington Marmaduke served in the Confederate army, and while camping across the river, he told his fellow officers he would one day live in the mansion.

All three people died during the holiday season and lay in state with the festive decorations. Who knows what causes the unexplained oddities that happen within the Governor's Mansion?

Missouri State Penitentiary

Opened in 1836, the prison underwent expansion until 1888. It was named the largest prison in the world and bore the nickname "the Wall." It established Jefferson City as the capital of Missouri and was the oldest continuously operating prison west of the Mississippi River when it closed in 2004, to be replaced by the modern Missouri State Correctional Facility. After almost 170 years of operation, the possibilities of paranormal activity seem promising. Several visitors since the prison opened for tours have seen a woman wearing gray in the women's prison area on more than one occasion. Riots occurred in the 1950s, and a series of assaults occurred in the early 1960s, earning it the reputation of being one of the most violent prisons in the country.

With its notorious history and number of deaths on-site, the prison is ripe for ghostly visits. Murders took place inside the walls. One inmate was chased through the courtyard by another wielding a shank. The unfortunate man was backed against the wall in the flower bed and stabbed to death.

Several notorious inmates served time inside the state penitentiary. Sonny Liston learned to box while in the prison, where public boxing matches were held periodically.

James Earl Ray Jr., the man who assassinated Martin Luther King Jr., was held in the housing unit.

A dungeon is beneath the housing unit; half was converted into showers, but the untouched portion still holds shackles. Inmates were held for months in the large, cavelike cells in total darkness, a practice that often resulted in permanent blindness. A gas chamber is part of the new tour, located in a small building outside the courtyard. Thirty-nine people were executed in the gas chamber, and now visitors can see the site that claimed so many lives.

In its 168-year history, the penitentiary played host to various notorious criminals.

On December 25, 1895, "Stagger Lee" Shelton shot and killed William Lyons in St. Louis in the Bill Curtis Saloon. The crime Lee Shelton committed would become the basis for the murder ballad "Stagger Lee." After two trials, Shelton was convicted and sent to the state penitentiary on October 7, 1897. He helped the prison officials capture a "systematic thief" and had the support of a few powerful Democrats in the state, helping him to gain parole close to Thanksgiving 1909. Shelton was later convicted of robbery and assault and returned to prison on May 7, 1911. He was ill with tuberculosis, and after a failed attempt at a pardon, he died in prison on March 11, 1912, and was buried in an unmarked grave in St. Louis.

"Pretty Boy" Floyd robbed a Kroger store/warehouse in St. Louis on September 11, 1925. He was described as being a "pretty boy," and the nickname stuck. He was given a three-and-a-half-year sentence. Once he left the state penitentiary, he headed to Kansas City and robbed banks. On June 7, 1933, Floyd is rumored to have linked up with Vernon Miller and Adam Richettil; they attempted to free Frank Nash from federal custody.

Four officers and Nash wound up dead in what became the Kansas City Massacre. Floyd denied any role in the massacre. In October 1934, he was tracked to a farm in Clarkson, Ohio, and killed in a shootout with law enforcement officers.

Sonny Liston was convicted in 1950 of armed robbery in St. Louis and sentenced to five years in the penitentiary. Liston took up boxing while in prison. He was paroled after two years, and on September 25, 1962, he knocked out Floyd Patterson in the first round, making him the heavyweight champion of the world. He held the title for two years, until February 25, 1964, when he quit against Cassius Clay (who later took the name Muhammad Ali).

James Earl Ray Jr. was incarcerated in the Missouri State Penitentiary after robbing a Kroger store in 1959. He was a habitual offender and was sentenced to twenty years. In 1967, he worked in the prison's bakery and squeezed into a four-by-four box. Another convict layered bread on top of the box, and it was loaded onto a truck leaving the prison. Guards failed to conduct a thorough search, and Ray escaped on April 23, 1967. One year later, on April 4, 1968, Ray assassinated Dr. Martin Luther King Jr. in Memphis, Tennessee.

By 1954, the state penitentiary had gained a reputation for having the bloodiest forty-seven acres in America. The population grew to the point that six to eight inmates might be confined to a single cell. The prison was deteriorating and overcrowded, and a violent riot broke out on September 23. The event began in the maximum-security "E Hall," which housed the more violent criminals. After order was restored, four inmates were dead and three guards and thirty prisoners were injured. Eight buildings were destroyed or damaged by fire. Two minor riots followed a month later, on October 23 and 24, resulting in the death of another inmate and the injury of thirty-six others.

By the 1960s, a series of assaults made national headlines and brought attention to the prison. In between 1963 and 1964, there were 550 different accounts of assaults and hundreds of stabbings. A lack of administrative control from the warden was cited as the cause. E.V. Nash had been given the position after the riots of 1954 in the hope that he could restore order. This scandal brought about an administrative review and a report promoting the removal of Nash as warden.

On December 18, 1964, Warden Nash took his own life in a house directly across from the state penitentiary with a gunshot to his head.

Within the grounds stands one small building isolated in a fenced courtyard. Between the years 1937 and 1989, thirty-nine or forty prisoners were put to death inside this tiny, ominous chamber. All but one of the executions used cyanide gas pumped into the sealed chamber. George "Tiny" Mercer was the first man executed in the state of Missouri for the rape and murder of twenty-two-year-old Karen Keeten. There was a suspected leak in the chamber, and Tiny received a lethal injection on January 26, 1989. Mercer was the first execution after the 1977 reinstatement of capital punishment.

After being decommissioned in October 2004, several plans were developed to begin demolition on the buildings. The more historical buildings were spared the fate of others in September 2007, when demolition took place on various locations within the complex. Reports of paranormal activity surfaced only after the destruction of buildings at the site. Reports, vague as they have been, include cell doors slamming on their own, apparitions and laughter ringing out in the buildings.

There are also rumors suggesting that the facility is a UFO base. Several photos have been circulated showing strange lights and shapes hovering above the facility. Jefferson City is not the only Missouri location with report of UFOs. Lebanon, on I-44, has been a site of UFO reports. Springfield, Kansas City and Lake of the Ozarks have all had sightings. Montgomery

County, where I spent the majority of my childhood, was notorious during my teenage years for UFO reports. A classmate and her boyfriend spoke of not only seeing one but also being chased by it.

I watched unknown flying objects at sunset and after dark; these would remain completely still in the sky, with the entire object changing colors. The objects would move in quick motion, only to stop and hover and then fly upward, out of sight, at a forty-five-degree angle. Missouri contains more mysteries than simply the lingering dead.

SPRINGFIELD PLATEAU

1 Ounce fresh red clover blossoms
1 Pint boiling water
1 Cup honey

Boil blossoms in water and strain. Add honey; bottle.
Dosage: one teaspoon twice daily.

—Old folk remedy for whooping cough

The Springfield Plateau is lower than the Salem Plateau. In many areas, the plateau's surface, at an elevation of about eighteen hundred feet, forms extensive plains. Hilly areas occur, with rivers and tributaries cutting into the plateau's surface, most notably in the vicinity of the White River. Also, the Buffalo National River cuts through the plateau down to the level of the White River, carving spectacular bluffs.

Underlain by limestone and chert, a flintlike rock, the earth is easily dissolved by water, making cave and karst features prominent. Surface water drains directly into channels in limestone, moving rapidly and without filtration to the surface as springs.

South-facing, cherty slopes are occupied by shortleaf pine and hardwood forests. With extensive, fairly level areas, often blanketed with prairie that was easy to till, the Springfield Plateau was much easier to develop for transportation, agriculture and urban centers than the Boston Mountains.

Combining the scenery and quality of life of the Ozark Mountains with a relatively level topography readily developed, the Springfield Plateau has become a growth center, of significance not only in Missouri and Arkansas but nationally as well. This region extends into Oklahoma and a small portion of Kansas.

SPRINGFIELD

Drury University is well known for its ghosts; however, the general public may never get a chance to experience them. Drury University is a private liberal arts college located in Springfield, Missouri. Congregationalist church missionaries established it as Springfield College in 1873.

Drury opened its doors for classes on September 25, 1873, after being constructed atop Native American burial grounds. To make room for the city of Springfield, the Indians had been removed by the government and sent to a reservation in Kansas.

The site also experienced the Civil War and was once dotted with beautiful Victorian homes.

First came a two-story brick structure for classes, costing a mere $7,000. At that time, the campus occupied less than one and a half acres and had thirty-nine students.

Springfield, Missouri, on Route 66. Vintage postcard. *Courtesy Janice Tremeear.*

A frame building for the music department was built. In 1875, an elegant brick structure, called Walter Fairbank's Hall, was opened as a women's boardinghouse. Twenty-five years later, the forty-acre campus included Stone Chapel, the President's House and three academic buildings.

Today, it sprawls out over 110 acres.

Charlene Wells, a member of Route 66 Paranormal Alliance, supplied the following information on the ghosts of Drury:

Smith Hall, women's dormitory, was built in 1966 where several Victorian homes once stood. One of the houses had a sordid past and its own haunting: the little girl in pink who lived in the old Victorian. A house fire ignited one evening, raging out of control. The little girl, safely outside, dashed back to search for her teddy bear. She perished in the fire and now roams the halls of the women's dorm, still trying to locate her beloved toy.

She's a small child, all decked out in pink and reported to be quite mischievous. She prefers to pull her pranks on the second floor of the eastern hall, leaving dresser drawers pulled open. Locked doors are left standing wide open. If a student owns a teddy bear, the stuffed toy will often be found sitting in the middle of the room. Teddy bears throughout the dorm are moved from place to place, possibly left after the little girl played with them.

The little girl also touches people, and she has been caught in photographs. Once, an unused phone stored in a closet began ringing in the middle of the night with no power source to it. Even homework has gone missing, only to reappear after a polite question to return it was asked.

Clara Thompson Hall has an unknown ghost who plays the piano and opens and closes doors. The hall has a 450-seat auditorium and is home to the music department on campus. It was a gift to the university in 1925 from Louise Groesbeck Wallace, in memory of her daughter, Clara Wallace Thompson. A woman is said to walk around the halls at night. Could this be the piano-playing ghost?

Nearby, the soccer field, off Bennett Street, was constructed on top of scared Native American ground, bringing about numerous reports of unknown presences in the area.

"Bob" the ghost is the haunter of the 250-seat proscenium Wilhoit Theater, according to Charlene. "Students report lights within the theater flickering off and on at night, with no one present inside of the building."

FANTASTIC CAVERNS

Caves hold all the mystery of a haunted house, with the extra oomph of total darkness. Even with candlelight, the way many caves were explored in the days before flashlights, the darkness clung to the walls just beyond your fingertips or became a huge well of nothingness as the rooms grew larger or drop-offs lurked at your feet.

Northwest of Springfield hides one of the more than fifty-six hundred known caves in Missouri. Fantastic Caverns is one of the show caves still open for tours and is unique in being a cave through which you take a fifty-five minute tour in a jeep-drawn tram on a path left behind by an ancient underground river. The tram holds twenty-five occupants, who are encouraged to touch a particular section of low ceiling stalactites.

In 1867, a brave group of women armed themselves with ropes, ladders, torches and lanterns and ventured into the darkness of the unknown at the request of the owner.

A farmer, John Knox, whose dog chased an animal into the entrance in 1862, discovered the cave, crawling inside only far enough to retrieve his dog. Preventing the cave from exploitation by Union or Confederate soldiers, he kept the cave's existence quiet until 1867, keeping a possible source for saltpeter quietly hidden.

The women answered a newspaper ad to explore the cave, and their names are written on the wall as proof of their passage. Two weeks earlier it had been explored as well, but these ladies are considered the first since they left their names within the cave.

Prohibition brought new traffic into the cave, as the wide rooms became a gaslit speakeasy, which closed in the 1960s after a fatal shooting

A vigilante group (said to be the Klu Klux Klan) bought the cave to hold its secret meetings until it couldn't make the payments and lost the cave in 1939.

In the 1950s and '60s, dances and concerts were put on inside the cave, with a maintained temperature of sixty degrees year-round. It also hosted a weekly live radio show in the Auditorium room, which can seat several thousand people.

The name was changed to Fantastic Caverns during the 1950s, and it became a drive-through show cave during the '60s as more families came to the Springfield/Branson area for vacation.

Albino and blind, the Ozark cavefish, cave crayfish and grotto salamander share the same life, never seeing the sunlight. Unmindful vandals can easily endanger these creatures, as well as the cave features.

Ghosts in the cave are suspected to be that of a priest, an Indian warrior, smallpox victims and two men killed inside the cave. A young girl is seen wearing a polka-dotted dress at the first bridge crossover. Apparitions leaving contrails have been captured. Mist is spotted in the speakeasy area, orbs are caught in photos and EVPs include chanting.

My family took the tram ride through the cave. We stopped at the Auditorium room and had the chance to get out and stroll around the huge underground theater. I love caves in general, but the sheer size of the underground rooms at Fantastic Caverns was quite a treat and easily offered the mental image of an underground dancehall setting.

COBRAS IN SPRINGFIELD

Ghosts and UFOs are not the only unusual stories connected with the Ozark Mountains. Springfield gained the attention of *Life* magazine in an article titled "The Big Ozark Cobra Hunt" for its September 28 issue in 1953. The article outlined the strange events that took place on St. Louis Street (part of old Route 66) August to October of that year. Page fifty-one of the magazine tells that a report came in to the police about a snake being killed that couldn't be identified. The cobra struck out at Roland Parrish in his yard on East Olive, but Parrish hit the snake with a garden hose, killing it.

Vintage postcard. Walnut Street, Springfield. *Courtesy Janice Tremeear.*

Hooded cobras were found in buildings along Route 66, and the occurrence made national headlines. It became a media circus, with businesses advertising cobra haircuts, "cobra districts," a cobra cocktail and a song entitled the "Snake 'Em Out Blues."

The snakes came from an exotic animal store on St. Louis Street. A disgruntled teenager had bought a fish at the store and felt he'd been cheated when the fish died. Seeing a cage of snakes, he assumed they were harmless black snakes and released them.

"Anything can happen in the Ozarks," said the city commissioner after the first snake was found. Unaware of the cage of cobras released in the city, nothing more was made of the unusual incident at that time.

Across the street from Parrish, a neighbor's dog started barking. Its owner looked out from his house to see the dog in conflict with another snake and knew it wasn't a harmless black snake. Wesley Rose pinned the cobra down with a hoe until police arrived.

A local science teacher, Herbert Condrary, was called in. He took a look at the snake and said, "My God, that's a cobra!" The critter was a naja naja, a hooded cobra found in Africa, the Middle East and Southeast Asia, not typically between Glenstone and National in Missouri. The hunt was on.

"Snakes in Springfield" along Route 66. Vintage postcard. *Courtesy Janice Tremeear.*

120

Several snakes were seen after that. Some were killed, and others were chased beneath homes and smoked out by tear gas grenades. The area along Route 66 became known as "Little India."

Brush fires were set by a "cobra posse" on September 12; they netted a few lizards and a turtle. Cobras were run over by cars and beaten with rocks, and antivenom was shipped into town in case someone was bitten.

During this time, the kidnapping and murder of six-year-old Bobby Greenlease was making national headlines. St. Louis's Coral Court Motel served as a hideout for Carl Austin Hall and Bonnie Heady, Bobby's killers.

Cobras and Springfield shared tabloid front-page print with the Greenlease case as snakes continued to raise their hoods along St. Louis Street (Route 66). On October 5, a public address system outfitted on a truck rolled into town. Snake charmer music rattled through the system, and authorities waited for the vipers to be lured out into the open. "The Cobra Blues," however, did not work, since cobras have no ears. The press enjoyed the embarrassment of this attempt. A cobra did show up, slithering from beneath a house on nearby North Prospect—whether in response to the piped music or by happenstance, no one knows.

Cobra number eleven made its appearance on East Olive Street and was held for the police by David Kelley, who planted his foot on it head. Number eleven was the first snake taken alive. It was three feet long and was taken to police headquarters to later be sent to the Dickerson Zoo. The snake had its TV time and attracted a large crowd, but unfortunately it died in the zoo two months later.

In November, another snake made the news in Springfield, in conjunction, this time, with the trial of Bobby Greenlease's murderers. A seven-foot boa constrictor was discovered sleeping under the porch of Bill Dickey's house. Boas typically can't survive temperatures lower than fifty degrees, but this one had, since the temperature had dropped to twenty-six degrees before the snake was found.

Kerr Cemetery

Jeanna Barker is a member of Route 66 Paranormal Alliance and offers another tale of a haunted graveyard:

> *When I was in high school, it was a popular thing to go out to Kerr around Halloween. It was said to be haunted by devil worshipers from a very long time ago and their victims.*

One guy I knew, who was the most honest guy in town, came back from such a trip with a flat tire and a broken windshield. He said hooded figures jumped out in front of him. He stopped the car, then felt the car being attacked from all sides. He saw nothing behind him, so he drove in reverse till he was away from the cemetery. When he righted his car, he noticed the windshield had been broken, and by the time he got to town, his tire was flat. It scared him and his sister, but we went back out there in her car with him. We saw figures running toward us, and she sped up and got us out of there before we were attacked. The police investigated it when we told them—because we thought there were devil worshipers out there—but they found nothing and no trace of anyone having been in the cemetery all night.

HALLTOWN

Halltown was founded in the 1870s when George Hall opened the first store in the area. The post office was established in 1897 and named after Mr. Hall. During the heyday of Route 66, the town supported almost twenty businesses, including three grocery stores, a drugstore, a blacksmith shop, a service station, a garage and a variety store. Halltown was known as the "Antique Capital of the World."

"The Ghost Road" leaving Halltown on Route 66. Vintage postcard. *Courtesy Janice Tremeear.*

Today, few businesses survive, but boarded up stores sit quietly in this small town. One store that remains open is Whitehall Mercantile. A treasure-trove of antiques and collectibles sit displayed, floor to ceiling, in this long-standing building. First built in 1900 as a grocery and general store, with a stone foundation and wooden porch, the false-front mercantile offers a rich view of the past in both its building and its merchandise, which includes Route 66 memorabilia.

Other historic buildings making up Halltown include the 1930 Las Vegas Hotel and Barbershop and the old Hamilton Brown Shoe Company.

Ken Brewer relates a ghost story of Halltown; the exact location will remain unnamed to prevent vandals from destroying the property. A certain church in Halltown has been the site of a suicide. A man hanged himself in the balcony of the church, and now people report seeing "the body of a man through the upstairs windows. Sometimes a shadow is seen; at other times, the body, still swinging from the rope, is viewed from outside."

KENDRICK HOUSE, CARTHAGE

The Route 66 Paranormal Alliance joined with Lisa and Leon Martin, founders of the Paranormal Science Lab, for a tour and investigation of the historic Kendrick House on October 29, 2010, after I participated in a book signing along with Steve Cottrell, author of *Haunted Ozark Battlefields*. Charlene and I had been on an investigation to Kendrick before, but for the rest of the team, my son Nathaniel Wells and his stepsister, Amy Schechterly, it was a first.

Lisa sent me the following information about Kendrick:

> *Kendrick House was one of three antebellum homes to survive the two burnings of Carthage during the Civil War and is the oldest standing home in Jasper County. The home was occupied multiple times during the Civil War by both armies and by raiders. During the Battle of Carthage, it was used as the field headquarters and as a field hospital for Union troops. The two-story home was built between 1849 and 1854 with slave labor. The Kendrick family occupied the house for more than 125 years. In the beginning, it was a district conversation piece widely recognized as one of the finest residential buildings between the Mississippi River and the Rocky Mountains. Settlers found it particularly intriguing because it boasted a full complement of glass*

windows. The Kendrick mansion became a principal stopping point for travelers passing through the region. There have been reports of paranormal activity at Kendrick House over a long period of time.

Shadows are photographed at Kendrick. Voices are heard and objects are moved, and of course there are cold spots. A light in one of the upstairs bedrooms has been known to turn on by itself with no one present.

Kendrick was written up in *Missouri's Haunted Route 66*, and its appeal still holds. One of the spirits on the premises is assumed to be a young girl. She seems to be playful, ducking back and forth in front of cameras and video recorders.

Steve Cottrell, in *Haunted Ozark Battlefields*, says that Kendrick House first appeared in war records concerning the report of the July 5, 1861 Battle of Carthage as a detachment of Missouri State Guard cavalry passed over the grounds. The cavalry was on its way in a flanking movement during the battle.

But the raid by Confederates in the autumn of 1863 held a bigger role for the property. Colonel Joseph Orville Shelby rode into Missouri with one thousand troops to raid the Union forces controlling Missouri. As he

Kendrick House, Carthage. *Photo by Janice Tremeear.*

Foundation of the log cabin overlooking the Civil War battlefield, Carthage. *Photo by Janice Tremeear.*

advanced along the Missouri River, he destroyed many Federal supplies in the ten engagements he led before being turned back toward Carthage. Shelby set up camp at the Kendrick House near Spring River. Shelby and some of his men used the house as headquarters.

A strong Union cavalry rode from Carthage and captured a detachment of Confederates. Shelby sent five companies to confront the Union troops, and the battle raged in and around Carthage. Shelby and his troops were able to withdraw and continue their march back to Arkansas. This was called the Second Battle of Carthage. A haunting associated with Kendrick that doesn't include Civil War soldiers is the tragedy of the slave killed by marauders. The Jayhawkers also wounded another girl, who became the housemaid after being nursed back to health.

Carthage has a historic state site on the location of one of the last skirmishes of the battle of 1861, before Shelby's battle. The site encompasses the Carter Spring area, which is relatively unchanged since 1861. The First Battle of Carthage, also called the Battle of Dry Fork Creek, spread out over ten miles and was one of the first engagements of the Civil War. What is a city park now was the campsite for both armies, the Union the night before the battle and the Confederates the night after.

Colonel Franz Sigel led one thousand troops into southwest Missouri searching for Governor Claiborne Jackson and his company. When Jackson discovered that Sigel was in Carthage, he engaged Sigel's well-trained men in battle. Jackson's army consisted of four thousand armed but unorganized and inexperienced men and two thousand unarmed men who didn't participate in battle.

Sigel's army was eleven hundred strong and fully armed. The most severe fighting took place at Dry Fork Creek, Buck Branch and Spring River. The Confederate Missouri State Guard was victorious. The battle served very little purpose except to boost the morale of those citizens who were pro-South in their first victory.

We visited the site of the battle and were told of the vertigo others experienced at the location. Shadow figures are reported darting behind the trees here, and overwhelming unease and dizziness affects any who come seeking the spirits. Nathaniel felt the oppressiveness others reported from being on the very land where many were wounded. A dizziness seemed to come over several of those with us that night, and one woman wandered aimlessly toward a drop-off at the creek, unaware that she was heading for a tumble.

We wandered around in the dark, crossing the creek and climbing a hill to the remains of a home that was probably present on the day of the battle, the crumbling stone foundation bearing silent witness to the bloodshed a stone's throw below.

SOUTHWEST MISSOURI

Hanging a corn dolly in the chimney piece of a house brings good luck.
—Superstition

A popular family vacation spot is Branson, Missouri. Many of the towns around Branson sport ghosts brought about by the wild era of the Civil War and the atrocities that took place then, giving this popular vacation spot, with its hills and "hollers," an air of mystery. Given the violent history of the Native Americans, the Civil War, Baldknobbers, buried treasures from the days of marauders and even Spanish gold, southwestern Missouri holds morbid attraction beneath the surface of the music acts, water slides, mini golf and malls lining the "76 Strip" of Branson.

Then there's Alf Bolin and his horrendous acts at Murder Rocks. Bolin was about as low as a man could get. He skulked along the Springfield–Harrison Road to rob travelers. Credited with at least fourteen deaths (mostly old men and young boys), ranging from Forsyth, Missouri, to northern Arkansas, Bolin didn't join the ranks of men fighting during the war; he stayed behind to harass the families left to fend for themselves without men folk at home. One of his victims was twelve-year-old Bill Willis, who was carrying corn to feed a horse and was climbing over a rail fence with the corn. In cold blood, Bolin shot the boy dead. Another of Bolin's victims was an eighty-year-old man named Budd, shot while crossing the river with a wagon of corn to be made into bread. Apparently, many teenage boys joined the army just to seek safety from Bolin and his bushwhackers.

Bolin killed Union soldiers returning home, and rumors say they are buried at Murder Rocks (another example of the elephant rock clusters of granite exposed by the weathering away of soil).

Bolin caught wind of silver bullion shipping from the North to the Rebels in Arkansas and gathered his men—perhaps twenty total—to bushwhack the convoy and steal the silver (part of the treasure said to lay buried somewhere in the hills of Missouri).

Bolin made a mistake. He camped out at Layton Mill, near the home of a Confederate soldier, demanding food and shelter from the wife, Mrs. Foster, who was alone at the house. The Union army hatched a plan and offered Mrs. Foster a chance to win her husband's freedom in return for her aid. It sent Zachary Thomas to her house, undercover as a wounded Rebel soldier. Mr. Foster was a Confederate prisoner in Springfield, while Mrs. Foster was a Union sympathizer.

Bolin was suspicious of Thomas all evening, but he finally relaxed his vigilance after a large dinner, possibly of ham and beans. A colter had been set near the fireplace (a long, blade-shaped, homemade wedge of steel that attached to a plow to weigh it down to dig through tough roots and sod). Mrs. Foster said she was using it as a poker.

Bolin bent over the fire, and Thomas crushed his head with the heavy colter. Bolin's body was dragged into the back room, apparently dead. Then Bolin moved, and Thomas bludgeoned and stabbed him to death. Gunshots couldn't be risked with Bolin's men lurking outside.

When Bolin's body was brought to Forsyth, Missouri, his head was cut off and displayed on a pole. The head was later delivered to the town of Ozark in Christian County to confirm that Bolin was dead.

Today, a rumor persists that a headless rider can be seen at Murder Rocks, and it's suspected to be the ghost of Alf Bolin come looking for his severed head. His body was buried in an unmarked grave near Forsyth, but what happened to his head? Hikers hear whispers coming from the woods—is it the voice of Bolin?

Reed's Spring is a quiet town snug in the Ozark hills. Morrill's Pond is no longer used by travelers to "tighten up" their wagon wheels and is no longer a place for bushwhackers to raid the innocent.

Ghost Pond was the name used for what is now Morrill's Pond. It sat along the Old Wilderness Road, 120 miles long from Berryville, Arkansas, to Springfield, Missouri. The Wilderness Road crossed the White River where Kimberling City stands today, snaked up hills to Lynchpin (now Branson West), passed one hundred yards away from Ghost Pond and continued up past Railey Creek in Reed's Spring and on to Springfield.

Bushwhackers banded together to become 120 men strong with the intention of stealing livestock and other valuables to take to Arkansas to sell. They plotted at their encampment by Ghost Pond and then rode out, plundering the town of Galena and killing three people. One victim was named Baker, and it's said he refused to give up his wealth and was hanged by the gang. After the raid yielded 150 head of cattle and fifty horses, the bushwhackers headed for Arkansas.

The Stone County Home Guard was alerted, and the son of Mr. Baker joined in pursuit. Captain Baker and his lieutenant, Charles Edward Philibert (son of one of the first settlers, Joe Philibert), chased down the bushwhackers, catching them at Railey Creek. The Home Guard ran low on ammunition but was successful at running off the bushwhackers, who abandoned most of their ill-gotten goods.

Back at Ghost Pond, the gang rejoiced in outlasting the ammunition of the Home Guard, feeling they'd won a great victory. But the Home Guard regrouped and laid a trap. In the middle of the night, the Home Guard surrounded the bushwhackers at Ghost Pond and murdered the sentries. At dawn came the full-out attack. Firing at close range, the Home Guard slaughtered the still drowsy guerrillas. From 120 men down to 20, the surviving bushwhackers fled to the state line, harassed all the while by the Home Guard.

Bushwhacker bodies littered the way from Railey Creek to Ghost Pond, and the pond's name was changed to Deadman's Pond. Nine bodies were found floating in the water, while others were never recovered from the depths of the pond.

After the incident, word spread that cattle refused to drink from the pond because of the bodies beneath its surface. Spirits were reported at night. A human skull was found in the pond, wedged into a stump; bones, gun pieces and Minié balls were located when the land surrounding the pond was plowed.

Deadman's Pond is all but forgotten now, but the legends of the pond add to the air of mystery in the Ozark hills.

Branson

Branson draws thousands of tourists each year. Its humble beginnings came in 1882, when Reuben Branson opened a general store and post office at a riverboat stop. Branson was formally incorporated in 1912. Construction of

Historic downtown Branson. Postcard. *Courtesy Janice Tremeear.*

the Powersite Dam nearby on the White River, forming Lake Taneycomo, was completed, and more people were drawn into the area.

By 1894, William Henry Lynch had bought Marble Cave (renamed Marvel Cave) and charged visitors to see it. Hugo and Mary Herschend leased the cave in 1950, on a ninety-nine-year lease, and began hosting square dances.

The Herschend family modernized the cave with electricity and cement staircases, and in 1960, the Herschends opened Silver Dollar City, a re-created frontier town of five shops and a church. Actors portrayed the feud between the Hatfields and McCoys on the streets of the city. Silver Dollar City is a fifty-five-acre park built over the remains of the old mining town Marmaros (Greek for "Marble") at the entrance to Marvel Cave. The town contained twenty-eight residences, a hotel, a school and a pottery shop and furniture factory. When the Herschends bought the land, the foundations of Marmaros could still be seen.

Marvel Cave is accessed via a large sinkhole first discovered in 1500 by the Osage Indians. One legend tells of the ghosts of both an Indian brave and the bear that he was chasing. They fell into the sinkhole, man chasing bear (or perhaps bear chasing man), and together they haunt the caverns.

Adventurers later explored the cave in the 1880s after lowering themselves on ropes two hundred feet into the main chamber. One interesting stunt performed in the cave involved hot-air balloon rides inside the domed chamber beneath the sinkhole.

Civil War veterans formed a mining company, pulling out bat guano during the 1800s; however, no marble was discovered. The cave was featured in *Scientific American* magazine in 1885, and William Henry Lynch purchased the cave, sight unseen, after reading the account of its beauty.

Lynch was a mining expert, and along with his two daughters, he opened the cave to public tours in 1894. Lynch himself is one of the ghosts said to wander the darkened recesses of the cave today.

Harold Bell Wright visited the cave in the 1900s, and his book, *The Shepherd of the Hills*, published in 1907, garnered national attention and turned a spotlight on the southwest Ozarks. Other ghosts are said to roam the popular vacation attraction, often seen and photographed during the day.

Silver Dollar City was always a vacation spot for our family when my husband's workplace closed for the week of July 4. My cousin Daniel Rush was a woodcarver at the city, and his mom and dad would sing at the Wilderness Church during one of the city's festivals. Wanda played piano and Jim played guitar, and with Daniel on banjo they harmonized as only family can. Once on vacation, they called us up onstage. My girls, Jennifer and Charlene, and their dad and I all sang old-time hymns with them.

In 1969, Silver Dollar City drew national attention when producer Paul Henning brought the cast and crew of the popular *Beverly Hillbillies* television show to the park to film five episodes of Season 8, when the Clampetts return to their home. Henning was inspired to create the series after a Boy Scout camping trip to the Ozarks in 1962.

SHEPHERD OF THE HILLS

The Old Mill Theater opened with the Shepherd of the Hills Outdoor Drama & Homestead near Old Matt's Cabin, home of the shepherd himself from Wright's book. Inspiration Tower rises high above the tree line here. The advertised World's Largest Toy Museum and Harold Bell Wright Museum are here as well. So is the Lizzy McDaniel House, the oldest original building on-site.

The McDaniel House is the ticket office for those wishing to buy access to Inspiration Tower. Little do tourists know, when standing in line to hand

Lizzy McDaniel House at Shepherd of the Hills. *Photo by Dean Pestana.*

over their money, that the ghost of Lizzy herself may be looking down on them. She still resides in her home—at least, according to the people who've encountered her.

Dean and I roamed Branson, questioning the locals about ghostly lore. I knew about Shepherd of the Hills. I'd been there before on family vacations with my (now ex) husband and the kids. We took the tour of the homestead, including Old Matt's Cabin. There are claims that the cabin is haunted, but people I spoke with who work the homestead say they haven't encountered anything ghostly associated with the log cabin.

I've watched the play at the amphitheater and gone up in the tower when my cousin Wanda was employed at the homestead. Little did I know at the time, but the tower and the play are haunted.

During our visit to Branson, Dean and I went to Molly's Mercantile at the homestead. Darla Kelly and Tiffany Jussel shared what they knew about the ghosts at Shepherd of the Hills.

Darla said that she and a co-worker, Missy, both heard singing in the tower. I was confused, wondering why the tower would be haunted, but the girls agreed that the entire homestead is full of activity. They said that in the past a lot of things happened—a lot of deaths and bad things went down here during the time of the Baldknobbers' reign.

Shepherd of the Hills, Old Matt's Cabin (background) and Inspiration Tower, near Branson, Missouri. *Photo by Dean Pestana.*

Tiffany Jussel, a cashier at Molly's Mercantile, says her mom heard noises upstairs at Lizzy's, and a wad of paper was tossed down at her. The upstairs is roped off, only employees are allowed access, and no one else was there at the time.

Another ghost is of a twenty-year-old girl seen on the homestead. She met her fate by being run over by a golf cart.

The homestead goes by another name: Inspiration Point. One ghost in particular is quite famous.

During the season's run of the open-air play, a nightly visitor makes his appearance on stage with the cast of *The Shepherd of the Hills* play. He's been reported many times over, and the reports have always been the same. In one scene with a crowd of people, he is seen riding on his horse. The cast of course knows who should be present and who shouldn't, and this man is not one of the actors. Apparently, the reenactment of a certain scene triggers his appearance. It's thought that he was a sentry for the Confederates, on duty on the mountain ridge. No one knows why he's still here, but he was reported first in 1964 and has been seen since that time.

BALDKNOBBERS

Twenty-two years after Alf Bolin's reign of terror, a vigilante group, the Baldknobbers, was organized to protect women, children and the elderly from outlaws. Leftovers from the Civil War were a failing economy, high taxes, renegades such as Jesse James and the Youngers and general disorder. Minimal law enforcement could not hope to contain the outlaws ruling the isolated hills of southwest Missouri, and what authority was in place was generally set by family clans that elected and controlled the local sheriff. Outlaws seemed to always have relatives on the juries, and the vote would swing in their favor. The long-established code of the hills, originally dealing with conflicts, disagreements and outright disregard for law and based on moral and biblical beliefs, was no longer working.

The Home Guard that was formed to aid the people left behind during the Civil War often added to the distress of the time by helping itself to whatever supplies were needed from the towns and farms. The statutes of the code of the hills were enforced with methods of the times and accounted for the only real law and order.

Prior to the Civil War, Taney County saw only three murders, but from 1865 to 1885, between thirty and forty murders occurred. Only federal law officers could pursue criminals across state lines, and the few who were tried were acquitted by corrupt courts. The citizens of Forsyth thought that the lawless newcomers—composed of squatters, gypsies, vagabonds, outlaws and Confederates from the defeated South—should obey the laws of the town just as the law-abiding ones did. Not sharing the sentiment, however, the restless element openly showed their distaste for the law. Thus, conflicts arose, resulting in the formation of a citizens' committee.

Nathaniel N. Kinney settled in Taney County in 1883 and was appalled at what he found. Redheaded, tough-looking Kinney stood six feet, six inches tall and weighed three hundred pounds. As a former skull-cracking saloon owner and Civil War soldier, Kinney took no flack from any man. Kinney always wore two guns. He started a Sunday school and church service at Oak Grove Schoolhouse, preaching with his Bible placed on the homemade pulpit and a pistol on each side to show that lawlessness had to be stopped.

After another murder on September 22, 1883, Kinney put into practice an idea taken from other groups popular at the time. When the killer was acquitted by a crooked jury, Kinney gathered twelve men, leaders in the county, to meet in secret on Snapp's Bald, north of Kirbyville, Missouri.

In the 1800s, the trees were not covering the mountaintops as they are today. "Bloody Hill" at Wilson Creek's Battlefield, near Republic, was a bare knob, offering a good view of the valley. The same can be said for the elevated regions where the men who joined Kinney gathered. They gained the name "Baldknobbers" from the bald mountain knobs or hilltops where they met. A rider with a lit torch was easy to spot from below as he waved his signal to call the vigilantes to meet.

Word spread of Kinney's plan, and at least two hundred men answered Kinney's call to gather at Snapp's Bald on April 5, 1885. The charismatic Kinney was voted leader and carefully laid out the goals of the secret, oath-bound group. It is recorded:

> *The first meeting of the group, which came to be known as the Bald Knobbers, was conducted in an orderly manner with all occupations present, school teachers, carpenters, rail tie makers and local merchants. There were no campfires, no masks and no throngs of angry members. What there was at the meeting, however, was a determination that something had to be done and a willingness to do whatever necessary to work against the lawlessness.*

One hundred Baldknobbers broke into the Taney County jail to kidnap the Taylor brothers. Frank and Tubal Taylor were vicious and wounded a storekeeper in an argument over a pair of boots. John Dickenson, the storeowner, was a Baldknobber, and the Taylors' fates were sealed. After the mob broke into the jail, it took the brothers south of Forsyth and hanged them.

Some of the original Baldknobbers couldn't stomach the violence displayed and dropped from the group, but the vigilantes continued to grow, soon flourishing at between five hundred and one thousand members. New recruits were often coerced into joining. It's said that coercion took the form of threats, the killing of livestock and the disappearance of entire families. When livestock or property went missing, a Baldknobber invariably showed up later in possession of a deed to the goods.

Bundles of switches were left on doorsteps as a warning. Shooting matches broke out, and neighbors feared one another, never knowing who might be a Baldknobber and turn them over for a beating.

Other "Balds" were used as meeting places: the famous Dewey Bald (Stone County) featured in *Shepherd of the Hills* and Scissors Bald Mountain (Taney County). A hiding place in a circle of rocks on top of the Balds allowed Civil War soldiers to make bullets out of lead and provided a lookout to spot anyone who might interfere.

In a manner mirroring the Slickers, the Baldknobbers would catch their prey, strip him, tie him to a tree in the woods and beat him with a black snake whip or a hickory gad (a spear or wand), meting out upwards of two hundred lashes. Rumors of men being beaten to death have surfaced as old-timers break a vow of silence in regards to the activities of the vigilantes.

A uniform was adopted, with coats being worn backward or inside out and masks made of pillowcases, often black, with "horns" tied at the corners and decorated. There appears to be no racial motive for the Baldknobbers, as in the case of other vigilante groups, although the era of the Civil War and Reconstruction did mark a turning point in lynching violence across the United States.

They became "the law," punishing any deviant behavior, from drunkenness to "loose women," and often beat gamblers, wife abusers and couples they considered to be "living in sin." If a person was ill favored by a member of the Baldknobbers, he could wind up beaten for being "ornery."

A power play ensued, and the group split into two factions, those with Kinney and those against. Those against Kinney wanted him dead.

An Anti-Baldknobber gang was organized to protect the people from a gang that had gone out of control. Governor Marmaduke ordered both groups to disband in 1886.

The Baldnobbers gained the nation's attention, but the group remained within the boundaries of the Ozarks. It was described as the largest and fiercest vigilante group in America. After the Taney County group disbanded, the Christian County group conducted a raid on an innocent group of citizens, sparking an outcry from the nation's newspapers. In the mêlée, a mask was torn off, revealing the identity of one raider. The known raider was arrested and quickly gave up all twenty-five of the Christian County Baldknobbers.

National attention focused on the men arrested for the murders of William Edens and Charley Green. They were tried on August 22, 1887. Of those tried, only four were convicted to death: Dave Walker; Walker's son, William; John Matthews; and Matthews's nephew, Wiley. The others served time in the state penitentiary. Of the four convicted to death, records show that only three were hanged.

Kinney's lieutenants were responsible for the Christian County group, but Kinney is not suspected as having had a hand in that organization.

Nat Kinney's men are credited with killing more than thirty men and four women, but it's generally believed that the actual number is between fifteen and eighteen. The powder keg raged as firebrands glowed every night, and screams of the Baldknobbers' prey rang in the woods. Stories tell of women being molested by the Baldknobbers and children being knocked down by horses if they stood in the Baldknobbers' path.

Nathaniel himself gunned down one man who stood against him. Andrew Coggburn called Kinney the "Old Blue Gobbler" for strutting around like a puffed-up turkey. One day, as Kinney approached the Oak Grove School, Coggburn and a group of men stood to challenge him. After a quick draw, Andrew lay dying, and Nat Kinney was unharmed. But he was marked for death by the Anti-Baldknobbers.

"The Captain of the Baldknobbers," Kinney was killed on August 20, 1888, by Billy Miles. Some say he was a hired assassin. Another account says that Miles was harassed by Kinney to join the Baldknobbers; he was called out by the captain and then shot him in self-defense. Miles was tried for Kinney's murder and found not guilty. Legend says that Kinney's widow later hired assassins to kill Miles.

History seems confused concerning Captain Nathaniel Kinney's death. One can read that on August 20, 1888, Nat Kinney was shot and killed by Billy Miles, a member of the Anti-Baldknobbers, in a planned assassination. There are also statements saying that the Anti-Baldknobbers who were incensed over the abuse of power included Matt Snapps, Tom Layton, Monroe Snodgrass, Seck Cogburn and William Miles Jr. These men allegedly played cards in Colonel Almus Harrington's barn for the honor of killing Nate Kinney. Miles won, held good to the agreement and shot Kinney in August 1888 in a grocer's store.

Miles was tried for Kinney's murder but was found not guilty based on self-defense. (In another telling, Kinney was ambushed and killed by the Taylor brothers at a store he operated in Forysth. Kinney had caught the Taylors stealing horses.)

With the death of Captain Kinney, the Taney County Baldknobbers had lost their leader.

And in 1889, the last of the renegade Baldknobbers would be hanged in the town square of Ozark. The three men from the Christian County "Knobbers" were marched up to the platform. Hoods were draped over their heads, and the lever for the trapdoor was sprung. There was a problem, however. This was the sheriff's first hanging, and the ropes were too long.

All three men dropped through the trapdoor without breaking their necks. Their feet barely touched ground, and the three were slowly strangling to death. The sheriff went to one of the Baldknobbers and used his rope to pull him up off his feet until he died. The others thrashed around, and the sheriff grabbed another rope, trying to lift the man off his feet. Hangings drew the townspeople, and this one was no different. At the sight of the second man being swung up off the ground, many in the crowd fainted.

Grabbing the third man's rope, the sheriff tried swinging him off his feet, but the rope slipped off his head, along with the hood. The young man fell to the ground in pain, blood seeping from his mouth. He cried, "Get it over with!" The sheriff got the man back up through the trapdoor and replaced the noose. With another jerk of the lever, the door opened and the young man dropped. Again the rope was too long. The crowd screamed, and the boy dangled helpless. By now, the sheriff didn't have the strength to pull on the rope, and the young man was left to die slowly, choking to death after an agonizing sixteen minutes.

The reign of the Baldknobbers came to an end with that hanging.

Harold Bell Wright camped at Inspiration Point, overlooking Mutton Hollow, as he began to gather his characters and story for his widely popular book. The nightly presentation takes place on the J.K. Ross homestead, the couple who inspired the characters Uncle Matt and Aunt Mollie. Old Matt's Cabin has been restored with all of the original furnishings. Lizzy (Lizzie) McDaniels was one of first people to promote the site. She bought the homestead in 1926 and moved her house from Springfield to the farm. She would sit on the lawn of Old Matt's Cabin and read the story to spectators.

The outdoor production of Wright's book is presented with 85 percent of the dialogue straight from the book. The actors are all local amateurs, with the directors preferring little or no prior acting experience to maintain true Ozarkian characters.

The theater, just down the hill from Old Matt's Cabin and Lizzy's house, is built on the actual site of the Ross Mill, where in times past the community members gathered to have grain ground, visit and buy supplies they couldn't grow at home. Actors portray the story from a real-life landscape that

Above: The author at the Lizzy McDaniel House at Shepherd of the Hills. *Photo by Dean Pestana.*

Below: Photograph of *The Shepherd of the Hills* play at Inspiration Point. *Photo by Dean Pestana.*

includes the mill, the shepherd's cabin (set ablaze with every performance) and a square dance.

On a tour of the homestead, I was told that the road for the play was actually part of the "Old Trail Nobody Knows How Old." While large enough on the stage for several horse-drawn wagons and buggies to maneuver, it narrows to run through the spit-sized village of Notch, Missouri, where Levi Morrill, who was the model for Wright's character Uncle Ike, ran the post office.

Night passage for people on horseback involved carrying lanterns or torches, and one can imagine the darkness of the Ozark night while taking the tram ride through the woods behind the gift shop up on Inspiration Point's hill.

Branson has grown considerably, and a lot of the older attractions are gone. I can no longer see the "Jim Lane Cabin" at the edge of the "76 Strip", since the new theaters have swallowed up the land. But a certain rustic appeal still lingers, like one of the ghosts left over from the days of Alf Bolin, the Civil War or the Baldknobbers. Thirteen counties in southwest Missouri and northwest Arkansas institutionalized the "playground" notion of the area, organizing the Ozark Playgrounds Association in the fall of 1919. Publicity encouraged tourism, and the slogan "the Land of a Million Smiles" became the catchphrase.

The Ozarks' rusticity was a critical part of the Arcadian paradise imagery (associated with bountiful natural splendor, harmony, utopia), and the mystics of the White River country said the pure Ozark mountain air held special, magical powers to induce good health.

Some places billed themselves as health resorts, and promoters boasted of the healing effect that Harold Bell Wright experienced, himself as an urban tourist who sought respite from poor health in the hills. And Levi Morrill (Uncle Ike) came to Stone County (it's said) after being told he only had a few months to live. In a short time, he tossed aside his canes and lived thirty-three years longer than expected, to the ripe age of ninety.

Pearl Spurlock is another who benefited from the pure air and operated a taxi service. In her book about the Ozarks, she tells the story of great-great-grandsons waiting for the patriarch to die so they could collect their inheritance. At 145 years of age, they took him away from the Ozarks to Chicago, where he promptly expired. The family brought him home for burial, and the Ozark air resurrected him. He died later of natural causes, and his heirs had him interred in Chicago to prevent him from a second resurrection.

Perhaps this explains the ghost among the Ozark hills. The air is not as pure as when Wright came to the area, but the idea of utopia still draws crowds and may still give life to those long gone. The rider at Inspiration Point may just be there to remind us of the reason people settled in the Ozarks in the beginning.

ARKANSAS

A grandfather clock stopping by itself, while the weights are high,
means a death in the family.
—Superstition

Earliest man reached back to about 10,000 BC. These people were bluff dwellers, with homes in caves and beneath overhanging rock cliffs along the White River. These ancestors to Indians included the Plum Bayou people living in east central Arkansas. They built eighteen platform burial mounds, some aligned to coincide with the summer solstice and fall and spring equinoxes. One mound was forty-nine feet tall. Five are still visible. They abandoned their land for unknown reasons. Among the earliest inhabitants of Arkansas were the Folsom people, who lived here when the last of the great glacier ice sheets was melting off the northern part of what is now the United States.

The Parkin people and Nodena tribe both vanished shortly after Hernando de Soto passed through their territories in 1541, possibly due to the white man's diseases. A drought also occurred that might have played a role in the demise of the native tribes.

The Arkansas were the forerunners of the Quapaw. The Tunican people occupied southeast Arkansas and were few in numbers. Another tribe to survive the European epidemics was the Caddo.

Mound Builders lived farther south, with the most significant Stone Age monuments belonging to the Toltec people in Lonoke County. These original inhabitants of Arkansas disappeared for reasons that are unclear. Other Indians living in Arkansas were the Osage, Choctaw, Folsom and Cherokee.

By 1835, those groups had been forced to leave, making way for settlers of European descent. Temporary waves of Native Americans driven from eastern states flooded through Arkansas to join with the indigenous tribes. In the late 1830s, members of eastern tribes crossed Arkansas as part of the forced exodus known as the Trail of Tears.

Arkansas was formed from the territory purchased in the Louisiana Purchase. The early Spanish or French explorers of the state gave it its name, probably a phonetic spelling of the Illinois word for the Quapaw tribe.

Arkansas refused to join the Confederate States of America until after the attack on Fort Sumter, South Carolina, and President Abraham Lincoln called for troops. Unwilling to fight against its neighbors, the state seceded from the Union on May 6, 1861, and was the site of numerous small battles. The Union captured Little Rock in 1863, and the town government relocated to Washington in the southwest part of the state. One of the most brilliant minds of the Civil War was Arkansas-native Major General Patrick Cleburne. He was referred to as the "Stonewall of the West." Major General Thomas C. Hindman was also noteworthy and commanded troops at the Battles of Cane Hill and Prairie Grove.

BOSTON MOUNTAINS

The babies of the plateau region of the Ozarks are the Boston Mountains. They were born about 300 million years ago and are the most rugged, rising to twenty-seven hundred feet. This highland has the greatest relief of any formation between the Appalachian Mountains and the Rocky Mountains. The region developed its own lifestyle. Mountain people occupy the narrow valleys and ridges. Like the rest of the Ozarks, this rectangular-shaped area, twenty to thirty-five miles wide and two hundred miles long, is a popular recreation spot.

Several peaks, including Turner Ward Knob and Brannon Mountain, exceed twenty-four hundred feet and with wide, gorgelike valleys, embrace a division of the Ozark National Forest, Buffalo National River and Devil's Den State Park, Arkansas.

The rocks in the Boston Mountains are nearly all sandstone and shale that were deposited during the Pennsylvanian era, approximately 290 to 323 million years ago. The sandstone was deposited in two environments. The older sand beds were deposited by streams that flowed across the continent to an ancient ocean south of what are now the Boston Mountains. The younger sand beds were deposited at sea level in delta channels as water inundated the land. Between the sandstone layers lies thick shale. The older shale beds were deposited on the flood plains beyond the stream channels. The younger shale beds were deposited in swampy areas between the delta channels and in the marine environment beyond the deltas.

This ancient coastline was permanently lifted high above sea level approximately 300 million years ago, during the collision of the North American and South American continents. The brunt of the collision and the resultant folding and faulting of the rocks occurred south of the Boston Mountains area, so there is minimal folding and faulting of rocks in the Boston Mountains. However, this uplift has allowed streams to erode deeply into these flat-lying rocks.

Eureka Springs

Several locations in Arkansas became famous for the fresh, bubbling waters issuing from the cool caverns and clear streams. Eureka Springs was a major draw for people from all over the country to partake of the "healing waters" during the 1800s. Aches, ailments and pains were all

"The Narrows," Eureka Springs, Arkansas. Vintage postcard. *Courtesy Janice Tremeear.*

thought to be eased or even cured by the spring waters, which could be bottled and shipped across country.

Railroads added to the influx of people seeking relief, and the same Ozark air that was reputed to have bestowed such healing on Harold Bell Wright and Uncle Ike near Branson highlighted the appeal of the hill country.

A railroad spur from Seligman, Missouri, to Eureka Springs by the Frisco Railroad accommodated the tourists flooding the area. Liveried footmen waited at the railroad depot to transport guests to the Crescent and Basin Hotels.

The city of Eureka Springs was founded and named on July 4, 1879. By late 1879, the estimated population of Eureka Springs had reached ten thousand people, and in 1881, the town was declared a "City of the First Class," the fourth largest city in Arkansas. Today the entire downtown area is listed on the National Register of Historic Places.

CRESCENT HOTEL

One of the most famously haunted hotels in America is in Eureka Springs, Arkansas. Like a king sitting on his throne, gazing down on his subjects, the seventy-eight-room Victorian Hotel perches atop West Mountain, one of the tallest peaks in the area. Dating back to 1884, the Crescent Hotel and Spa drew in the wealthy from all over the United States before air conditioning made summer bearable. By the late nineteenth century, those who could afford to do so left the hot cities for the cooler climate of seashores and mountains.

Built between 1884 and 1886 by the Eureka Springs Improvement Company, the hotel possibly gained its first ghost when a red-haired, Irish stonemason named Michael lost his footing and fell off the roof during construction. He landed in the second floor, where the infamous Room 218 is located. Michael plays with the lights and TV, pounds from inside the walls or pulls pranks on hotel guests. Hands have been seen coming out of the bathroom mirror, and cries of a man falling from the roof are heard. One guest reported blood splattered over the walls of the room, and he refused to stay the night. Michael apparently has shaken one guest out of a deep slumber, too. A couple of friends of mine stayed in the room the night before one of them was to be married. Carol Cummings witnessed the bride's long hair being pulled up and away from her head by unseen hands.

"Bird's Eye View" of Eureka Springs, Arkansas, with the Basin Park Hotel in the foreground and the Crescent Hotel in the background (on the hill). Vintage postcard. *Courtesy Janice Tremeear.*

The designer for the grand hotel was Isaac L. Taylor, well known in Missouri as an architect and famous for a number of buildings in St. Louis. His fame grew from his work at the St. Louis World's Fair in 1904. Mr. Powell Clayton was a financier for the Crescent and became governor of Arkansas from 1868 to 1870.

At a cost of $294,000, the spa sits on twenty-seven acres and became the stopping place for people traveling on the Frisco Railroad. Heavy magnesium limestone was moved from the quarry on White River to be used in the construction of the Crescent.

The hotel sported architectural touches giving it unique features. Numerous towers, overhanging balconies and eighteen-inch-thick granite walls lend an ominous and foreboding air to the gothic mystery of the building. The lobby remains fitted with a massive fireplace, and in the original construction, electric lights, plumbing and bathrooms were set in place. At one time, over five hundred guests could be seated in the Crystal Dining Room.

Dr. Baker's Extraordinary Bistro and Sky Bar on the fourth floor tops the décor, designed by Dr. Baker himself in his semi-deranged color pattern of purples, orange, black, yellow, silver and reds during the time he ran the hotel as a cancer hospital (1937–39).

Outside, gazebos, boardwalks, flower gardens, tennis courts, croquet and a swimming pool enticed the wealthy to the Victorian-style village with the "healing springs" that boasted such curative qualities.

On May 20, 1886, a gala ball heralded the grandiose Crescent Hotel's debut in a midst of fanfare.

The *Eureka Springs Times Echo* christened it "America's most luxurious resort hotel." Notables across the United States arrived for its grand opening, complete with a full orchestra and banquet dinner for four hundred.

The brand new spa catered to the rich and famous for over twenty years, offering grand balls and use of the stables with one hundred sleek horses. Ladies rode sidesaddle in their long skirts and veiled hats, while the elegant gentlemen rode alongside, cantering over the trails on early morning rides.

Other entertainments included afternoon tea dances, parties each evening, an in-house full orchestra and excursions down into the picturesque town of Eureka Springs. Streetcar rides, hiking and picnics rounded out the activities.

The Tally Ho was a large open coach drawn by teams of four, six or eight horses, and the Tally Ho rides to Sanatorium Lake were always popular.

Flourishing until 1907, the Crescent was taken over by the Frisco Railroad, which leased the property as a summer hotel. Then people began to realize that the springs were pleasant but not the "heal-all" cure advertised, and the gilded age aristocrats moved on to other pursuits. A decline in Eureka Springs tourism had its affect on the Crescent over the next sixty years.

Never completely abandoned, the hotel became the Crescent College and Conservatory for Young Women in 1908, an exclusive school for wealthy young ladies. A summer crowd still visited the hotel, but the tourist season was not enough to pay the bills, and tuition for the college climbed. The school closed in 1924 before returning briefly as a junior college (1930–34).

During the hotel's stint as a college for proper young women, a tragedy occurred. One young lady was said to have thrown herself from one of the balconies, seeing suicide as the answer to being jilted by her sweetheart.

The "dark days" of the hotel came about in 1937, when a new owner, Norman Baker, turned the building into a hospital and health resort. "Dr." Baker had a checkered past. He was once a star mentalist on the vaudeville circuit in the early 1900s. He was not a physician, but he touted a nonsurgical procedure relying on tea composed of commonplace ingredients.

Crescent Hotel "Castle in the Air," overlooking Eureka Springs. Vintage postcard. *Courtesy Janice Tremeear.*

He was the inventor of the Tangley Calliaphone in 1910. This organ operated via air pressure instead of steam. Unfortunately, Baker was not satisfied with the millions made from his organ, and his false notion of being a medical expert resulted in many fake cures and conspiracy ideas that the established medical field was not only hampering the sale of his cures but was also out to kill him.

Baker launched the KTNT (Know the Naked Truth) radio in Iowa in 1925 and published *TNT* magazine. He made attacks on the American Medical Association on air and in print over established medical procedures. President Herbert Hoover helped Baker's newspaper, the *Midwest Free Press*, in 1930 by taking part in a publicity stunt, turning a golden key in Washington, D.C., to start up Baker's printing press.

Baker first owned the Baker Institute in Muscatine, Iowa, but came under the scrutiny of the American Medical Association. It pulled his license in 1931 and issued a warrant for his arrest for practicing medicine without a license. Baker fled to Mexico and hid out there for several years. In 1932, and still a fugitive in Mexico, he ran a campaign for governor of Iowa.

By now, the Federal Radio Commission had shut down his radio station, so he opened a cross-border station, XENT, to promote his campaign. His Iowa hospital was shut down after he was sued, and he moved his cancer patients to Eureka Springs.

Upon his return, he took control of the Crescent, the "Castle in the Sky," and converted it into the new Baker Hospital, with his highly advertised "cure for cancer" attracting folks across the country.

He painted the hotel in garish colors and destroyed the wooden handrails. For a time, Baker pulled in a lot of money from people seeking a cure; however, his claims were bogus, and many people died at the hospital. A morgue was established in the basement of the hotel, and bodies were shipped out to the railroad station during the night. The autopsy table and freezer are still within the hotel. (Note: some accounts list the third floor as the area for the morgue.)

Baker was arrested in 1939 and charged with mail fraud in 1940 for his mail-order claims that "guarantee to cure cancer." He had promised his patients that drinking the spring water would save them, and no X-rays or operations would be performed.

After his trial, he served four years in the Leavenworth Federal Penitentiary. Baker Hospital closed. His apartment was found outfitted with machine guns as wall décor and secret passages hidden in the purple painted rooms to keep him safe from the attack he fully expected from the American Medical Association.

Ghosts roaming the corridors match the date of operation for Baker's Hospital. Witnesses see the greedy Dr. Baker himself, dressed in a purple shirt and white linen suit. The sour-looking Baker is found in the basement, near the Recreation Room and on the first-floor landing.

A nurse, dressed in white, is seen pushing a gurney on the third floor. She's seen after 11:00 p.m., when the bodies were removed from the hospital, and she vanishes at the end of the hallway. Sounds of squeaking and rattling seem to "roll" down the hall. The laundry room was on the third floor, and at night the washers and dryers are heard turning on and off.

Another ghost walking the palatial grounds is Miss Theodora. Some say she cared for terminal cancer patients during the Baker Hospital days. Others claim she introduces herself as one of the cancer patients and is most often seen by housekeepers in Room 419. Her voice has been captured as EVPs.

The antique switchboard continued to receive calls from the empty basement until it was disconnected.

A distinguished, mustached Victorian gentleman is seen sitting at the bar or at the bottom of the stairway. Complete with formal attire and top hat, he remains quiet, never responding to questions until he simply disappears.

In 1972, new owners breathed new vitality into the hotel shortly after a fire gutted the fifth floor and a majority of the fourth. Urban legend says that caches of skeletons have been located within the walls of the hotel, and somewhere on the property are jars of preserved body parts. This tale has all the markings of a top-notch Hollywood horror film. The jars were hidden so that potential buyers wouldn't be frightened off by the body pieces. This adds to the creepy quality shrouding the "Grand Lady of the Ozarks."

More ghosts share the Crescent. In the Crystal Dining Room, paranormal activities run the gambit from Victorian apparitions to 1890s dancers in full attire. One Victorian gentleman is quoted as saying, "I saw the most beautiful woman here last night, and I am waiting for her to return."

A Victorian bride and groom have been seen in the dining room's mirror. Christmas packages are moved from beneath the tree, and chairs are rearranged to form a semicircle facing the tree. Once, all the menus were strewn about the room.

In the guest rooms, blankets and sheets are pulled off the beds while guests are sleeping. Objects move, and electrical appliances go on by themselves. People have been touched or pushed.

A small boy is seen skipping in the kitchen. Often, the pots and pans fly off the hooks of their own accord.

A young female from the college days is seen. Her screams are heard as she jumps, or is pushed, to her death. Rooms 202 and 424 have apparitions, and a ghostly waiter appears in the hallway carrying a tray of butter.

Other apparitions include a weeping woman who carries her child's blanket; a lady in the garden; a handsome man who knocks on room doors to ask people if they're waiting for him; a teenage boy who collapses, disappearing on the floor; a boy with thick glasses wearing knickers; a lady with a beautiful hat; a hooded figure; a man with a crooked smile; and the face of a man wearing a bowler hat.

There are cold spots, orbs and voices on recordings, as well as mysterious sounds. One guest reported being held down by her legs and arms and being suffocated. This was followed by the smell of sulfur and sweat, and something grabbed her ankles to pull her halfway down the bed.

Disembodied voices have been heard coming from the dining room.

TV's *Ghost Hunters* filmed at the Crescent. A thermal camera captured a full-bodied apparition. This thermal camera is able to "see" heat signatures of objects.

What causes so many spirits to reside at the Crescent? The urban legends that list the remains of Dr. Baker's patients being hidden on the premises also conclude that he experimented on the brains of the dead, as well as the living. These claims say that his cure for brain tumors was to peel away the scalp and pour a mix of spring water and watermelon seed directly onto the patient's brain. Of the dozens of people who died on-site, the bodies were disposed of by incineration at night. His "incurable" cases would be confined to an asylum to cover the fact that he had no cure. These are all tall tales, of course, handed down over the years. And one can imagine the person bearing the story of the hidden body parts and brain surgery wringing his hands together and laughing in the best movie villain's "bwaa haa haaa" voice. The brooding hotel just lends itself to the fabrication of fantastic stories, adding to the sordid history of its days as a cancer hospital.

BASIN HOTEL

"Boo at the Basin" is the motto for the hotel on the north side of Basin Circle Park. Sitting on Spring Street in the downtown building district is the sister hotel to the famous 1886 Crescent Hotel and Spa. Built in 1905, the Basin Park Hotel has an eerie paranormal history of its own. It was built on the site of the Perry House, a four-story hotel constructed in 1881.

Captain Joseph Perry built the hotel after moving to Eureka Springs because of poor health. He owned several hotels in different locations across the United States prior to his arrival here. The Perry House, lost in the fire of 1890, was considered a fine hotel.

In the Victorian historic district in downtown Eureka, the Basin is listed on the National Register of Historic Places. The hotel is next to cold water Basin Springs, at the heart of the health resort community one hundred years ago. Basin Park Hotel is constructed of white limestone and pink dolomite rock walls built into the side of a mountain. All eight levels of the hotel are at "ground level." This unique feature earned it a place in *Ripley's Believe It or Not*.

During the Prohibition era, Joe Parkhill, a wheeler and dealer, promoted tourism to Eureka Springs by encouraging the law to turn a blind eye to illegal activities. He owned the Basin Hotel.

The sixth-floor Rooftop Billiards Room was equipped with slot machines and a long bar that served liquor, both illegal during this era. The signs of illegal activity could be quickly hidden behind doors, marked storage, in the event of a surprise police raid.

Word of this unique illegal venue in the scenic, hidden mountain town spread to Chicago. Chicago was home to gangsters, who were attracted to the remote mountain town. These men made the hotel one of their hangouts. It is rumored that Al Capone's sister stayed at the Basin Park Hotel for over a month.

Tourists at Basin Park in Eureka Springs, near the Basin Park Hotel. Vintage postcard. *Courtesy Janice Tremeear.*

The Basin Park Hotel attracted shady characters and their cohorts in the 1940s and 1950s to partake of parties and illegal activities.

The construction of the hotel, with every floor having a ground entrance, provided a quick escape route from every room. This unique characteristic was perfect for a quick escape from a fire, and gangsters found it ideal for a quick escape from the law when necessary.

The hotel had one hundred rooms, a cage elevator, electric lights, steam heat, telephones in the rooms and complete fire protection. On the top floor was a ballroom with a hardwood floor that was often referred to as the "Roof Garden." In later years, the Barefoot Ball became an annual event, with live bands during the 1940s, and the tradition continues today, with guests dancing shoeless.

Notorious lawbreakers from Chicago thought the Basin Park Hotel, with its easy access to illegal activities, was a great vacation getaway. Joe Parkhill registered many guests at no charge. The arrangement apparently worked for the involved parties.

In 1955, a new sheriff decided to put an end to the criminal element in Eureka Springs. Police raided the Barefoot Ball after the liquor and slot machines had been broken out. Joe Parkhill, John Doe and Jack Rabbit were arrested and taken to jail. All slot machines were smashed.

Without booze, the Chicago "friends" lost interest in Eureka Springs.

Basin Park Hotel and Park, Eureka Springs. Vintage postcard. *Courtesy Janice Tremeear.*

Parkhill found the hotel hard to operate without booze and gambling, so he sold the Basin Park Hotel to a retired United States congressman and Eureka Springs native, Claude A. Fuller.

Congressman Fuller had owned the Basin Park Hotel and the 1886 Crescent Hotel in the 1920s. He sold the hotels in 1931, a couple of years after he was elected to Congress. Now, once again, the hotels belonged to Fuller.

Eerie sights greeting visitors include a phantom dog, ballroom ghosts, a lion ghost, a translucent woman with cotton candy hair and steel blue eyes, a brown-suited man and a risqué room.

One man was in asleep in bed with his wife. He awoke to see a pale young girl walking through the wall. The young girl lifted the covers of the bed. The man was frozen in fear, yet his sleeping wife never woke during this nocturnal ordeal.

Reported sightings of a little girl around the age of three or four, with pigtails and a yellow dress, tantalize those seeking to capture her on camera. Odd noises are heard. Various other strange happenings are commonplace. Apparently, some guests have never checked out, as evidenced by floating orbs, pool cues flying off the walls and people being touched.

Today, the Basin Park Hotel features Serenity Day Spa, a swimming pool, the Lucky 7 Rooftop Billiards Parlor and front-door access to over one hundred unique downtown shops.

Overlook at Mount Judea (Mount Judy), Arkansas. *Photo courtesy Dean Pestana.*

MOUNT JUDEA

A small town in Arkansas is the gateway to a recreational area with an interesting history. Mount "Judy," as it's called, is the site of a former stage stop with a headless ghost. A gambling room upstairs was the scene of a brawl that ended in a man being decapitated. Legend says that you can still hear the argument and the head bouncing down the stairs. Dean Pestana has gone to Mount Judy and Sam's Throne on several occasions, and he told me the sad story of a lost boy who roams the area.

SAM'S THRONE

This legend dates back to the 1820s. Buffalo hunter, farmer and firebrand evangelist Sam Davis roamed Arkansas' valleys in Newton County, searching for a sister he claimed Indians had captured. Davis scrambled to the top of the tall sandstone butte every morning and yelled mighty sermons to the hardscrabble settlers living in the valley below. Sam proclaimed he would live a thousand years.

Sam's Throne near Mount Judea (Mount Judy). *Photo by Dean Pestana.*

Besides spewing damnation, Davis claimed to have a hoard of gold stashed on the summit of his rock, and he built a log blockade across the formation's walkup to keep out would-be thieves. Moonshine and Sam's rumored treasure earned the mountaintop the name of Sam's Throne.

The ghost story surrounding Sam's Throne is of a lonely Boy Scout who died in the woods and is buried in there. It is said that the apparition of a young boy can be seen running through the woods.

BIBLIOGRAPHY

Angus, Fern. *Superstitions of the Ozarks and Deep South.* North Little Rock, AR: Jenkins Enterprises, 2006.

Belekurv, S.M. *2012: The Paranormal Cookbook.* Springfield, MO: MEC Publishing Company, 2009.

Cheung, Theresa. *The Element Encyclopedia of Ghosts and A Haunting.* London: Barnes and Noble in association with Harper Collins Publishing, 2008.

Cottrell, Steve. *Haunted Ozark Battlefields.* Gretna, LA: Pelican Publishing, 2007.

Delano, Patti. *Off the Beaten Path: A Guide to Unique Places.* Guilford, CT: Globe Pequot Press, n.d.

Gilbert, Joan. *Missouri Ghosts.* Hallsville, MO: MoGho Books, 2001.

Keister, Douglas. *Stories in Stone: A Field Guide to Cemetery Symbolism and Iconography.* New York: MJF Books, 2004.

Little Giant Encyclopedia—Superstitions. New York: Sterling Group, 2001.

Patton, Phil. *Open Road: A Celebration of the American Highway.* New York: Simon & Schuster, 1986.

Randolph, Vance. *Ozark Magic and Superstition.* N.p., n.d.

Show Me Route 66 20, no. 4 (2010).

Terry, Dan. *Beyond the Shadows.* Stanton: Missouri Kid Press, 2007.

Weaver, H. Dwight. *Lake of the Ozarks, Vintage Vacation Paradise.* Charleston, SC: Arcadia Publishing, 2002.

———. *Missouri Caves in History and Legend.* Columbia: University of Missouri Press, 2008.

ABOUT THE AUTHOR

B orn in St. Louis, Missouri, Janice is one of the founders of Route 66 Paranormal Alliance, and she and her team travel, researching all aspects of the paranormal—not only ghosts but also cryptids and other unexplained phenomenon. They use methods such as old-fashioned dowsing (the old-timers called it "water witching") and modern means via electronic equipment and research. Janice is a member of MUFON (Mutual UFO Network) and the author of *Missouri's Haunted Route 66: Ghosts Along the Mother Road* (The History Press, 2010) and *Wicked St. Louis* (History Press 2011). She writes for the FATE-sponsored Spooky Southcoast website and was instrumental in the concept for developing a media format that would generate original programming, such as paranormal mini episodes, for WEBX Radio.

Janice is active in lecturing on haunted locations along Route 66 and in Missouri and was one of the guests at VisionCon 2011, Springfield, Missouri's sci-fi, anime and gaming conference. The Route 66 Paranormal Alliance was the first paranormal team ever invited to participate at VisionCon.

Photo by Dean Pestana.

Visit us at
www.historypress.net